Winesburg, Ohio

AN EXPLORATION

Twayne's Masterwork Studies
Robert Lecker, General Editor

Winesburg, Ohio

AN EXPLORATION

Ray Lewis White

TWAYNE PUBLISHERS • BOSTON
A Division of G. K. Hall & Co.

Twayne's Masterwork Studies No. 55

Copyright 1990 by G. K. Hall & Co.
All rights reserved.
Published by Twayne Publishers
A division of G. K. Hall & Co.
70 Lincoln Street
Boston, Massachusetts 02111

Copyediting supervised by Barbara Sutton.
Book production by Janet Z. Reynolds.
Typeset in 10/14 Sabon
by Compositors Corporation, Cedar Rapids, Iowa.

First published 1990.
10 9 8 7 6 5 4 3 2 1 (hc)
10 9 8 7 6 5 4 3 2 1 (pb)

Printed and bound in the United States of America.

Library of Congress Cataloging-in-Publication Data

White, Ray Lewis.
    Winesburg, Ohio : an exploration / Ray Lewis White.
      p.   cm. — (Twayne's masterwork studies ; no. 55)
    Includes bibliographical references.
    ISBN 0-8057-8097-1 (alk. paper). — ISBN 0-8057-8136-6 (pbk. : alk. paper)
    1. Anderson, Sherwood, 1876–1941. Winesburg, Ohio. 2. Winesburg (Ohio) in literature. I. Title. II. Series.
PS3501.N4W579   1990
813'.52—dc20
                                        90-4209
                                          CIP

In honor of

Hilbert H. Campbell and *Charles E. Modlin*

fellow explorers

Contents

Note on the References and Acknowledgments

I wrote a long time ago that I believe in genius because, most unexpectedly, a poorly educated ex-manufacturer in middle age suddenly wrote several exquisite stories about important but hitherto ignored citizens of an imaginary but nevertheless quite real Ohio town in the 1890s. I still believe in the special genius behind Sherwood Anderson's *Winesburg, Ohio* stories, and I still enjoy writing about and teaching these marvelous fictions from 1919.

After studying, teaching, and writing about *Winesburg, Ohio* for over a quarter century, I am indebted to all others who have written about it, and I could not possibly acknowledge each and every student, historian, and critic to whom credit is due for the ideas that he or she has shared with me and that have influenced my perceptions of Anderson's work as expressed in this book. I therefore simply thank all who have written and talked about Anderson's masterwork since its publication on 8 May 1919, and I limit the Notes and References herein to only those writings in history or criticism that expand most usefully upon the topics I raise in my discussion.

The best text for reading *Winesburg, Ohio* is that prepared by Malcolm Cowley (New York: Viking Press, 1960). My parenthetical textual references herein are to the 1976 Penguin Books edition, which is based on the text presented by Cowley in 1960. The reader who wishes a close approximation of the somewhat rare 1919 first edition of *Winesburg, Ohio,* however, can find it in any Modern Library version of the work in its many printings since the 1920s.

Portions of this book originally appeared as "Of Time and

Note on the References and Acknowledgments

Winesburg, Ohio: An Experiment in Chronology," *Modern Fiction Studies* 25, no. 4 (Winter 1979–80): 658–66. © by Purdue Research Foundation, West Lafayette, Indiana. Reprinted with permission.

SHERWOOD ANDERSON
Courtesy of the Illinois Historical Society

Chronology: Sherwood Anderson's Life and Works

1876   Sherwood Berton Anderson born 13 September in Camden, Ohio, the third of seven children of an improvident harness-maker and a hardworking homemaker.

1884   Anderson family moves to Clyde, Ohio, the town where Sherwood grows up, attends school, and holds many part-time and, after elementary school, full-time jobs to support the family. The town later becomes a kind of model for *Winesburg, Ohio.*

1895   At the mother's death, the family breaks up. Sherwood travels to Chicago, where he finds work as an unskilled laborer in cold-storage warehouses and the like. Attends night classes in business subjects.

1898   Leaves Chicago to serve in Cuba (after combat ends) in the Spanish–American War.

1899   Moves to Springfield, Ohio, to complete a high school education at the Academy of Wittenberg College, where he makes helpful contacts in business and advertising.

1900   Returns to Chicago to work as an advertising copywriter and solicitor. Begins writing essays about business for an advertising journal and later essays about literature for another magazine.

1904   Marries Cornelia Lane, well-educated daughter of an Ohio manufacturer, and continues working in Chicago and writing about the advertising profession.

1906   Moves to Cleveland, Ohio, to operate a goods-distribution company and makes his way successfully as an entrepreneur. Aims at financial greatness.

1907   Moves to Elyria, Ohio, to operate another goods-distribution company and to continue an upwardly mobile life. In Elyria, the last of his three children is born.

1909   Starts writing fiction (which remains long unpublished) about unhappy manufacturers and financial moguls who need personal and sexual liberation.

1912   Disillusioned with business and under psychological pressure, is afflicted late in November by aphasia, amnesia, or "fugue state" that hospitalizes him and ends his Ohio business career and his traditional family affiliation.

1913   Returns to Chicago to earn his living by writing advertising copy; also writes fiction as part of the city's artistic group. Becomes acquainted with Carl Sandburg, Edgar Lee Masters, Harriet Monroe, Margaret Anderson, Francis Hackett, Ben Hecht, Floyd Dell, and other Chicago Renaissance figures.

1914   Discovers the stylistically avant-garde writings of Gertrude Stein. Publishes "The Rabbit-Pen," a traditional story, in *Harper's* and, in various "little magazines," less traditional stories and essays about writing.

1915   Unhappy with writing derivative fiction, is in the winter suddenly inspired to write "Hands," the first *Winesburg, Ohio* story. Successive stories about Winesburg come into being over many months.

1916   Is divorced from Cornelia and marries Tennessee Mitchell. Continues writing advertising copy and stories. Publishes his first novel, *Windy McPherson's Son,* about an industrialist who has wealth but not happiness.

1917   Publishes his second novel, *Marching Men,* in which the hero finds meaning through organizing laborers into potentially effective unions.

1918   Publishes *Mid-American Chants,* free-verse regional poetry reminiscent of Whitman and Sandburg. Lives in New York City and writes movie publicity. Seeks publication of the Winesburg stories as a book.

1919   *Winesburg, Ohio* published 8 May; reviews are mixed and sales scant.

1920   Lives briefly in Alabama and then in Palos Park, Illinois. Publishes *Poor White,* a novel about the industrialization of the Midwest.

1921   Visits Europe and meets Gertrude Stein and other writers. Publishes new stories as *The Triumph of the Egg.* Wins the *Dial* prize of $1,000 for his stories. By mail, introduces the young

<table>
<tbody>
<tr><td></td><td>Ernest Hemingway to Gertrude Stein and other authors in Europe.</td></tr>
<tr><td>1922</td><td>Finally abandons his work as an advertising writer and leaves his second wife and Chicago for New York City. Meets Elizabeth Prall, a bookstore manager and daughter of a successful merchant.</td></tr>
<tr><td>1923</td><td>Publishes Many Marriages, a novel about sexual liberation, and Horses and Men, a collection of stories. Lives in Reno, Nevada, to obtain a divorce from Tennessee.</td></tr>
<tr><td>1924</td><td>Marries Elizabeth Prall. Moves to New Orleans, where he advises young William Faulkner. Publishes A Story Teller's Story, his first autobiography.</td></tr>
<tr><td>1925</td><td>Publishes a financially successful novel, Dark Laughter, about psychological freedom. Visits the mountains of southwestern Virginia, where he buys a small farm.</td></tr>
<tr><td>1926</td><td>Publishes Tar: A Midwest Childhood, an autobiographical novel, and Sherwood Anderson's Notebook, a collection of essays. Settles on his farm near Troutdale, Virginia, where he builds Ripshin, his only permanent house. Very briefly visits Europe, where he is depressed, uncomfortable with Hemingway, and uncommunicative with Stein.</td></tr>
<tr><td>1927</td><td>Becomes owner, reporter, writer, and publisher of the two small Smyth County, Virginia, newspapers, the Marion Democrat and the Smyth County News. Publishes A New Testament, prose poetry.</td></tr>
<tr><td>1928</td><td>Meets and falls in love with Eleanor Copenhaver, daughter of a prominent family in Marion, Virginia, and a career social worker with the National Young Women's Christian Association.</td></tr>
<tr><td>1929</td><td>Publishes Hello Towns!, an anthology of small-town newspaper writings. Separates, despondent and perhaps suicidal, from Elizabeth.</td></tr>
<tr><td>1930</td><td>Begins traveling secretly with Eleanor to observe and write about labor conditions in southern manufacturing towns.</td></tr>
<tr><td>1931</td><td>Publishes Perhaps Women, a treatise on women's potential to redeem men facing the difficulties of modern life.</td></tr>
<tr><td>1932</td><td>Is divorced from Elizabeth and continues courting Eleanor. Travels to a radical labor conference in Europe. Publishes Beyond Desire, a political novel about southern labor organizing.</td></tr>
<tr><td>1933</td><td>Travels across America to observe and write of depression-era social conditions for Today magazine. Marries Eleanor.</td></tr>
</tbody>
</table>

Publishes his last collection of stories, *Death in the Woods.* Begins writing his final memoirs.

1934   Publishes *No Swank,* appreciative essays about his literary friends and their books. Continues to write social essays.

1935   Publishes *Puzzled America,* collected mostly from his *Today* magazine social essays.

1936   Publishes his last novel, *Kit Brandon,* about mountain moonshiners. Continues writing his memoirs.

1937   Publishes *Plays: Winesburg and Others.* Continues writing his autobiography.

1938   Visits and writes about Mexico. Continues his memoirs.

1940   Publishes *Home Town,* an illustrated treatise on the vanishing American small town and the best traditional American values once found there.

1941   Dies 8 March, in Colón, Panama, while traveling with Eleanor to visit and write about life in South America. Leaves his memoirs unfinished.

1942   Eleanor publishes the heavily edited and much-rewritten *Sherwood Anderson's Memoirs* and begins her duties as her late husband's heir and literary executor. She continues this work (while employed in the labor movement until her retirement in 1961) until her death in 1985.

1

Historical Context

On 13 September 1915 Sherwood Anderson turned thirty-nine. He was living in Chicago for the third time, writing advertising copy to support himself while trying to become a novelist. He had come to Chicago for the first time in 1896, after his mother died and his family scattered from his hometown of Clyde, Ohio. In 1898, ambitious for the riches promised to believers in the American dream—the faith that both wealth and happiness will inevitably come to the moral and the industrious—he had been able to find only exhausting and ill-paid manual labor in commodities warehouses. The disappointed young Anderson had eagerly left Chicago to serve in the U.S. military occupation of Cuba during the Spanish–American War and, after that military adventure, had completed his high school education at the Academy of Wittenberg College in Springfield, Ohio. In 1900, armed with both his old ambition and his new education, he returned to Chicago to achieve—surely, this time—his expanded and enriched American dream: to work in the new business of advertising, to marry the beautiful daughter of a rich manufacturer, and to someday control his own business firm and have power in his community and the nation.[1]

In 1906, having married the daughter of a rich manufacturer,

1

Anderson left Chicago for the second time, ready to become president of the United Factories Company in Cleveland; in 1907 he headed the Anderson Manufacturing Company in Elyria, Ohio. (Both companies manufactured little and were really distribution firms.) In late November 1912 he wrote his wife a confused note about striving in America and mumbled to his secretary some puzzling words about walking too long in the bed of a stream. Sherwood Anderson then walked out of his company office and wandered over the roads and fields of northern Ohio for four days, a victim of amnesia, aphasia, or "fugue state." He soon recovered in a Cleveland hospital, but he had completely lost interest in his failing business, his family (three children had been born), and his dreams of wealth and power. Early in 1913, he had returned to Chicago once again, alone, ready this third time to succeed as an artist and to make his recent trauma into a literary legend. He now claimed it to have been the considered, deliberate rejection of a great career in business rather than the psychological collapse of a deeply troubled man.[2]

Liberated in middle age from the usual responsibilities of family and business, Anderson took up (without enthusiasm) his old profession of writing advertising copy, by which he would make his living into the 1920s. But the Chicago to which Anderson returned in 1913 had an exciting and attractive new cultural aspect: the Chicago Renaissance in American letters. This wonderful but brief flowering of literary preeminence in America's second city between 1910 and 1920 produced such wonderful magazines as *Poetry: A Magazine of Verse* and *Little Review;* the shocking but influential new poetry of Carl Sandburg and Edgar Lee Masters; the innovative and satiric novels of Ben Hecht and Floyd Dell; a whole network of plastic and performing artists and their rich patrons; and the local journalists and enthusiasts necessary to declare the greatness of the new spirit of the arts that was alive and thriving in Chicago.[3]

Perhaps as early as 1909, Anderson had somehow decided that he preferred writing novels to writing promotional copy for businesses and playing in the world of ideas to playing in the world of country club golf. By the time of his nervous collapse in 1912, he had already drafted at least parts of several novels, writing at night in the attic of his home. These works had been of no interest to publishers and were the source only of amusement or confusion to his business associates. Taking the manuscripts to Chicago in 1913, Anderson showed them to his new young Chicago Renaissance friends. They encouraged him to rewrite and publish them and to write more fiction and poetry. Still, these unpublished literary efforts must surely have appealed to Anderson's Chicago friends more as the surprising products of an ex-manufacturer than as the admirable work of a new and vital creative writer.

In the autumn of 1915 Anderson was living alone in a roominghouse on Chicago's Near North Side, writing advertising copy by day and prose fiction by night. On one night in the winter of 1915–16, he almost magically—and certainly mystically—created his first piece of true literature.

The process of writing *Winesburg, Ohio* was for Sherwood Anderson the greatest event in his life, the miracle that confirmed his dedication to the creative act. While he always recognized the importance to his career of the book's publication, he later wrote most often about the actual composition of the work. He worked on his memoirs intermittently from 1933 until his death in 1941; perhaps the introspection and retrospection required in writing them caused him to exalt the composition of *Winesburg, Ohio*. Or perhaps his 1933 visit to the Chicago room where he had first known the joy of successful storytelling inspired him to glorify the writing of *Winesburg, Ohio*. Standing once again in his small room in the roominghouse at 735 North Cass Street (now Wabash Avenue) where he had lived alone in the winter of 1915–16, Anderson recalled sharing the house with some "Little Children of the Arts"—unknown men and women who wanted to become successful musicians, sculptors, painters, actors, and writers. As the oldest of the would-be artists in the house, Anderson had tried to write novels, poems, and essays that captured human life with their webs of words, but the art he created had not been art good enough to meet his drive and his desire. Then one evening during the winter of 1915–16, after a long day writing advertising copy, Anderson sat down at his table in the shabby little room and simply wrote from his heart the story of a little man who had been attacked, beaten, and twisted by life. The writing was unlike anything Anderson had read. The story was told in the ordinary words of everyday life and depended not on mere plot but on true psychological insight for its impact. In his *Memoirs,* Anderson recalled:

> The story was written that night in one sitting. No word of it ever changed. I wrote the story and got up. I walked up and down in that little narrow room. Tears flowed from my eyes.
>
> "It is solid," I said to myself. "It is like a rock. It is there. It is put down. . . ."
>
> I am quite sure that on that night, when it happened in that room, when for the first time I dared whisper to myself, perhaps sobbing, that I had found it, my vocation, I knelt in the darkness and muttered words of gratitude to God.[4]

Although Anderson's memory of the passion of writing "Hands," his first *Winesburg, Ohio* story, seems valid, his statement that he had to do little revision on it or on the stories that came to him in a similar manner in 1916–17 is suspect. These manuscripts show considerable revision by the author in diction, modification, suggestion, and specificity. But still, as Anderson always claimed, there is little evidence of revision in concept or theme.

As he composed story after story about Winesburg and its imagined inhabitants, Anderson perhaps thought of trying to publish them in the mass-circulation periodicals of the day. But only a few of the "little magazines" devoted to discovering and displaying daring, exciting new talent would accept stories that (for the time) were so revolutionary in telling and so distasteful in content. Nine of Anderson's stories about the imaginary town appeared in such historically important but then obscure magazines as *Masses, Seven Arts,* and *Little Review.* By 1918, Anderson had written almost two dozen stories about Winesburg, Ohio, and its peculiar citizens. He wished to collect and publish them as a book titled *The Book of the Grotesque,* and through a bold and innovative New York City publisher named Ben Huebsch, his collection of Ohio stories did appear on 8 May 1919 as a book—retitled by the publisher, with Anderson's consent, *Winesburg, Ohio: A Group of Tales of Ohio Small Town Life.*[5]

Nineteen-nineteen was the best year that Sherwood Anderson could have published *Winesburg, Ohio.* A few years earlier, the book would have been censored, suppressed, and maligned; a few years later, other works of literature would have served as American storytelling's liberating models, if perhaps less salubrious ones than Anderson's short stories were.

For World War I had ended in 1918 with great American elation at its victories on the battlefields of Europe, despite the late entry—in April 1917—of the United States into the war. From present-day perspective, the reasons for waging World War I seem pitifully inadequate in the light of the costs of the war. Between 1914 and the armistice on 11 November 1918, the Allied powers—including the United States—mobilized 42 million troops, of whom at least 5 million died, at a cost of $145 billion. The Central Powers, principally Germany, mobilized 23 million troops, of whom 3.4 million died, at a cost of $63 billion. The indirect additional costs to both sides amounted to at least $40 billion. This tremendous expense in human beings and money was for causes now important to no one except historians.

And with the war, American society had undergone the most rigid censorship, political suppression, and loss of human rights ever imposed in its history. Dissenters were jailed and fined; magazines and newspapers were shut down; political and economic radicals of leftist persuasions were hated and mistreated. All this governmental dictatorship was imposed by President Woodrow Wilson—the very same intellectual and idealistic man who as a candidate in 1916 had promised to keep the nation out of Europe's war.

The great American citizenry had enjoyed a great war victory at a relatively small cost in American lives. (53,515 U.S. troops died in battle, 63,195 died otherwise, and 204,002 were wounded.) After the war, they continued the self-righteous and chauvinistic behavior that alone, they thought, had carried them happily and steadily and profitably through the war months. A loosening of Victorian moral standards was opposed, as even prohibition of the drinking of alcohol became law. Radical labor leaders continued to be silenced and imprisoned for their beliefs, and the rebellion of youths who doubted that this war had made their world any safer or happier was fiercely silenced.

For the victorious American nation had a very pressing new fear, a new threat from Europe: in October 1917 the Bolsheviks had seized control of Russia, formed the Soviet Union, and immediately threatened to lead the masses of the whole world away from such godly American institutions as free enterprise, private property, and capitalism and into communism. So even after World War I ended, freethinkers, dissenters, and rebels were curbed in public and private life, and innovators in art and literature were discouraged from experimenting and from daring to create new forms or express new thoughts.

The first mechanized war in history had involved more of humanity than any other war. Afterward, nineteenth-century virtues and values seemed grossly inadequate and inappropriate, and a young "lost generation" of survivors of the battlefields and the home front sought new, nihilistic principles by which to live and to create. Into this uncertain if financially successful world came Sherwood Anderson's little book of stories. These stories were appreciated by freethinking, innovative readers and were admired and emulated by valiant and experimental writers. They gave postwar American fiction a new guide and model that was powerful and honest enough to encourage the proud, rich, and triumphant society that World War I had brought into being toward literary greatness.

2

The Importance of the Work

If William Dean Howells and William Sydney Porter had never been successful writers, Sherwood Anderson might never have written any stories about Winesburg, Ohio. For Anderson heartily despised what these two famous literary men had done, through their example and through their influence, to American writing in the early twentieth century, and his own writing was a response and a challenge to their influence.

Howells (1837–1920) was an Ohioan of the generation before Anderson's. As an editor of the *Atlantic Monthly* and then as a critic for *Harper's Magazine*—the two most influential literary periodicals of his day—he had two most respectable pulpits from which to propound his taste in literature. He spoke for the genteel, polite tradition in fiction, a tradition whose timidity and blindness to many important aspects of actual human behavior exasperated Anderson. His taste at least eschewed fantasy and escapist writing, but too often it could not expand to appreciate and encourage in the United States the kind of innovative and daring writing that was being published by realists and naturalists in Europe. Anderson, after his momentous psychological breakdown in 1912, could no longer countenance belonging to the respectable, middle-class, conservative society that Howells represented. Freed by his traumatic breakdown from the restraints of social and family life that he had so eagerly embraced as a businessman since 1900, he sought a liberation in literature that would be as salient as his liberation from established American values in his personal life had been.

Even before his November 1912 nervous collapse, Anderson may have forsworn allegiance to Howells and the genteel literary tradition represented by Howells, Henry James, Edith Wharton, and their imitators. Anderson later wrote that when he criticized to someone Howells's taste and practice in fiction, the listener challenged him to outdo Howells and publish in *Harper's* a better story of his own. Anderson's story "The Rabbit-Pen," published in *Harper's* in July 1914, was his rejoinder.[6] Whether this was its origin or not, "The Rabbit-Pen"—dealing with a reserved, timid, and aesthetic writer who is unable to understand or cope directly with his attraction to a strong German servingmaid who deals with a sexual crisis among the family's rabbits—outdoes most of Howells's writings in sexual and psychological innuendo. Since it was probably written before Anderson's breakdown, the story is a fair marker of his sensitivity to dominant literary taste when for some years he had already been trying to write novels in the attic of his Ohio home.

Howells's most direct and compact expression of his theory of writing is found in *Criticism and Fiction* (1891), a book of essays first published in *Harper's*. In chapters 21 and 24 of this book, Howells wrote that American novelists had reached a satisfactory solution to the problems of subject matter and purpose. They had perhaps once wished for the freedom of the European novelist to indulge in such matters as adulterous loving and forbidden thinking. But the reality of American life, wrote Howells, called on American authors to take a more polite and cautious approach to subject matter. Since fresh, new American life was more refined and proper than the decadent old life of Europe, American writers should properly concentrate their attention on the *typical* aspects—the cleaner, clearer, more pleasing aspects of American life. American writers should therefore never create any character or write any word that would offend the taste or the morals of the most innocent American girl who might chance upon them.

The Importance of the Work

In Ohio, Anderson had come to know more and more surely that Howells's and his literary followers' perception of American life was false. It denied the darker, dangerous, and more daring impulses of the human mind—impulses such as hatred, repression, vengeance, dominance, despair, anomie, perversity, and destruction. Anderson, having rebelled against middle-class life and its self-imposed blindness to the desperate aspects of life, could no longer countenance writing that strove merely to reassure the comfortable and to comfort the self-deceiving. His own fiction, should he manage to create any, would deal with the lives of the frustrated, the obscure, the cast-out, the violent, the deranged, the ignored, the distorted, the grotesque—in short, the characters, drawn from real American life, of whom William Dean Howells and the genteel tradition would not have approved.

The other dominant influence on American writing that Sherwood Anderson most heartily resented was that of William Sydney Porter (1862–1910), who as O. Henry had published to immense popularity over two hundred short stories. These stories set as in concrete a method and a tone for story writing that stifled originality and that for many years killed any development toward true greatness in the American short story. The appeal of the cheap and easy O. Henry short story remains so strong that it can yet distract readers from appreciating fiction based on true observation and artistic merit. Anderson frequently referred to the O. Henry story as the "poison-plot" story—the story that dwelled so obsessively on plot cleverness, especially on an unexpected "surprise" ending, that observation and presentation of actual human characters were of secondary or tertiary importance.

Told in a style that mixes polite colloquialism and pretentious, unusual words, the representative O. Henry short story seeks surface delight and avoids exploring the unusual and eternally interesting aspects of human behavior. A typical O. Henry story is "The Last Leaf," in which a self-indulgent young woman thinks she will die when the last leaf of autumn falls but survives the old painter who has kindly and secretly painted with oil a last leaf on her windowpane. Others include "Mammon and the Archer," in which a financial mogul secretly uses his money

to cause a traffic jam that allows his baffled son sufficient time to propose to an incredibly busy, beautiful, and rich young woman; "The Furnished Room," in which a young man, seeking his lost beloved in cheap
roominghouses, kills himself unknowingly in the very bed where she
died; and "The Gifts of the Magi," in which Della sells her beautiful hair
to buy her husband Jim a watch-chain for Christmas, while Jim unknowingly sells his watch to buy Della beautiful combs for her long hair. This
story of crossed purposes motivated by young love is relentlessly mora-
lized through seasonal sentimentality and allusion to the wise men who
allegedly brought gifts to the newborn Christ child.

To Sherwood Anderson, such superficial, easy, and popular fiction
simply would not do. With his own stories he sought to reform public
taste and artistic practice by demonstrating that life has depths and
darknesses unexplored by the genteel authors who agreed with Howells's
polite and cautious criteria for American writing or who followed O.
Henry into a meretricious sentimentalism that sugared over eternally pre-
dictable plotting. In 1919, with *Winesburg, Ohio* Anderson provided at
once a lesson and an example for fiction in which plotting was organic
and arose naturally from the material that was being created rather than
from received Procrustean formulae. With *Winesburg, Ohio* Anderson
made possible the exploration of the unusual, the bizarre, the outré, the
decadent, and the grotesque that for him made up the most interesting
and wonderful examples of human character. Subsequent American writers who achieved greatness in the short-story form—among them Ernest
Hemingway, William Faulkner, Thomas Wolfe, John Steinbeck, Erskine
Caldwell, William Saroyan, Flannery O'Connor, Carson McCullers,
Eudora Welty, and Katherine Anne Porter—owed much to Sherwood
Anderson's little book, a book that at once explored new subject matter
in the short-story form and that liberated that genre from old, rigid, and
artificial structures.[7]

3

Critical Reception

Sherwood Anderson continually wrote, even toward the end of his life, of the hurtful reception that readers gave *Winesburg, Ohio* on its publication in May 1919. In his final memoirs he wrote that the book "did not sell. It was widely condemned, called 'nasty' and 'dirty' by most of the critics. The book was more than two years selling the first five thousand. The condemnation of the book as nasty and dirty made me ill. For a long time I went about with my head hanging."[8] Anderson remembered further, "I wrote and published a book of tales, called *Winesburg, Ohio* and when it was published there was an outbreak of bitter denunciation. Letters kept coming to me, many letters, and they were all from women."[9] Elsewhere he recalled, "What names I was called. They spat upon me, shouted at me, used the most filthy of words."[10] And: "I remember that I had myself, upon the publication of my *Winesburg, Ohio,* been held, almost universally, in the public prints, as a filthy minded man and that after the book was published, for weeks and months, my mail was loaded with letters calling me 'filthy,' 'an opener up of sewers,' etc."[11]

But Anderson's avowed purpose in writing the *Winesburg, Ohio* stories had been to break the constraints of the genteel taste in American literature—the grip of W. D. Howells and O. Henry—that had stifled writers of his generation. There is therefore something disingenuous in his recollection of the reception of his masterwork. His daring in 1915–16 to write frankly of sexual repressions, thwarted desires, physical grotesquerie, and concealed loves and hatreds had clearly been meant to shock the comfortable literate bourgeoisie into a new conception of the proper subject matter for fiction—matter far more gross and offensive than popular taste had previously allowed.

Yet Anderson's recollection of some of the early reviews of his book was accurate. Said one reviewer, in a column invoking "a gutter," *Winesburg, Ohio* dealt with the "nauseous acts" of abnormal, perverted people. Anderson had taken worthwhile subject matter and changed it "from human clay to plain dirt."[12] Another reviewer wrote that, although Anderson had written a worthy story cycle, he would have to learn to censor his unnecessarily ugly plots and themes more strongly.[13] The author was complimented by a third reviewer for his "clear insight into character" that was, however, presented in a humorless and overwritten style, obsessed with neurotic characters.[14] A fourth reviewer appreciated that Anderson had avoided the Russian violence of Anton Chekhov but believed that the American nevertheless narrated his tales with a too-naïve simplicity and with a clear purpose of shock value.[15] A fifth reviewer, believing that Anderson's stories lacked obvious feeling and life, concluded that the author had written impressionistically and had somehow thereby buried the beauty of his created lives under realism.[16] These are the five extant negative American reviews of *Winesburg, Ohio* from 1919. Anderson remembered for the remainder of his life every unkind word that had been written early on about his story cycle but forgot the many positive comments made in 1919 about his stories and his technique.

For the other fifteen or so extant reviews of *Winesburg, Ohio* from 1919 say much that is wise and sympathetic about the volume. Maxwell Anderson (no relation to Sherwood) said that the author had given to American short-story writers a new form that could replace the old plot-story associated with O. Henry.[17] To another commentator, Anderson's stories tenderly revealed the deepest layers of human nature beneath the façade of ordinary small-town life, making of the author "an artist with vision and sensibility, with comprehension and the capacity to test reality with imagination."[18] Hart Crane, a fellow Ohioan who in 1919 had yet to be recognized for his poetry, wrote of *Winesburg* that Anderson showed flawless style, opening for readers "the windows, alleys, and lanes of the village . . . to find what epics, tragedies and idylls we may." The book to the nation "constitutes an important chapter in the Bible of her consciousness."[19] To Idwal Jones, a reviewer who sensed exactly what Anderson was trying to do with his stories, the work was "a revelation of men's motives by psychoanalysis, with the purpose of revealing that human existence is not necessarily a deadly commonplace, but that in every life there come, even if but once, moments of dramatic climax."[20] Llewellyn Jones, a Chicago writer who knew Anderson in 1919, wrote that in the Winesburg stories Anderson had treated "the significant episodes of lives" instead of creating only "well-constructed stories. His poetically told stories are frank revelations of small-town citizens without spiritual or sexual outlet."[21] H. L. Mencken, who had not yet made his reputation as a satirist of American life, wrote of *Winesburg, Ohio* that it created a new form for the short story—"half tale and half psychological anatomizing, and vastly better than all the kinds that have gone before."[22] And J.V.A. Weaver, a Chicago reviewer who was personally familiar with Sherwood Anderson, regarded *Winesburg, Ohio* as a literary work that did for America what Gogol and Dostoyevski had done for Russia, giving "a panorama, with souls instead of trees, with minds in place of houses."[23] While there were surely other reviews of *Winesburg, Ohio,* only these eighteen or so remain to gauge the reception of this book at its publication.

Anderson's memory of scant sales of his book in its first years of availability was absolutely correct. The work was reprinted several times by B. W. Huebsch, but all the early printings made up at most only a few thousand copies, and British publication added little to the sales figures. The book entered the Modern Library series of reprinted literary works and has thus remained in print in English continuously since 8 May 1919. Almost from its earliest years, *Winesburg, Ohio* has been accessible to millions of readers around the world, translated into Russian, French, Italian, Spanish, German, Danish, Portuguese, Swedish, Finnish, Czech,

Japanese, Chinese, Polish, Korean, Bulgarian, Hebrew, Greek, Hungarian, and Dutch.[24]

In retrospect, it can be seen that *Winesburg, Ohio* belongs to three different literary traditions at once, three approaches to fiction that were alive in the 1920s and that hold together for various readings of the stories. The first of these three traditions is that of "the revolt against the village"—exposés of the false and narrow values and the hidden unhappiness found in life in the American small town. After the agrarian myth—the idea that humans living close to nature on self-sufficient farms are the most moral and happiest of people—became outdated and impractical, the best human behavior was said to be found in the hamlet, village, or small town, where, far away from the known evils of the large and ever-tempting city, people could live in harmony with nature and with themselves. In reaction to this myth of small-town pleasures, the antithesis of the village pastoral emerged; in the 1870s the first American writings appeared that debunked wishful thinking about happiness in small towns: Edward Eggleston's *The Hoosier Schoolmaster* (1871), Mark Twain's *Adventures of Huckleberry Finn* (1884), E. W. Howe's *The Story of a Country Town* (1884), Joseph Kirkland's *Zury: The Meanest Man in Spring County* (1887), some of Hamlin Garland's stories in *Main-Travelled Roads* (1891), Harold Frederic's *The Damnation of Theron Ware* (1896), and—most important of all—Edgar Lee Masters's *Spoon River Anthology* (1915), that best-selling collection of small-town epitaphs in free verse. At the time of the publication of *Winesburg, Ohio,* these and other books epitomized American writing about the horrors of small-town and village existence.

But only to its loss is *Winesburg, Ohio* considered merely a player in antivillage literature, for Anderson did not hate his hometown of Clyde, Ohio, nor his imagined village of Winesburg; rather, he wrote lovingly and unsentimentally of the grotesque human characters that he imagined to be resident in Winesburg, and their fascinating artistic constructs as actors in literary tales. Anderson was clearly familiar with Masters's *Spoon River Anthology* at the time when he was writing *Winesburg, Ohio,* but although the two authors shared common subject matter, their approaches could not have differed more. Even more distasteful to Anderson was being categorized with Sinclair Lewis as a satirist of small-town life after the 1920 publication of Lewis's immensely popular *Main Street,* the quintessential novel about the American small town. Like Masters before him, Lewis was a satirist of American prejudices and blindnesses, but unlike Lewis, Anderson did not disparage or mock his creatures or their habitat in *Winesburg, Ohio.* Yet for years, Anderson's collection of stories was misread as another example of revolt against the American village. In this misreading, the central character of the *Winesburg* stories, George Willard, is a bright youth who well avoids the grotesquerie (and, I would add, the interest) of his more "distasteful" townsmen and townswomen.[25]

The second cultural tradition of the 1920s into which *Winesburg, Ohio* fits is that of literary naturalism. Theorized by Emile Zola in his treatise *The Experimental Novel* (1880), literary naturalism came to the United States and developed in the writings of the young realists who flourished around the turn of the century. In *Maggie: A Girl of the Streets* (1892) and *The Red Badge of Courage* (1895), Stephen Crane produced a kind of fiction in which human free will is an illusion; in which life is controlled by heredity, environment, circumstance, and accident; and in which values and beliefs are mere delusions of worried, uninformed persons. In Jack London's *The Call of the Wild* (1903), survival itself was the point of wild animal life and, by implication, of human life. Frank Norris in *McTeague* (1899) and *Vandover and the Brute* (posthumously published in 1914) took fiction about as far as it could go in animalizing the forces that determine human life. Theodore Dreiser in *Sister Carrie* (1900) and *Jennie Gerhardt* (1911) documented the aimlessness of life, life as nothing more than reactions of chemicals and electricity.

But *Winesburg, Ohio* differs from these naturalistic fictions that preceded it, for in Anderson's stories of small-town life, he discovered that the naturalistic determinants—the controlling factors of existence —inside his characters' minds were impulses more deeply buried than had been thought by earlier writers striving to fulfill Zola's prescription of an objective, scientific fiction.[26]

Anderson's more psychological determination of human character and destiny is the third 1920s and 1930s literary tradition into which *Winesburg, Ohio* fits—Freudianism. It is certain that Anderson read none of Freud's writings upon their appearance in English, beginning in 1910. But even before the American publication of *Three Contributions to a Theory of Sex* (1910), *The Interpretation of Dreams* (1913), *History of the Psychoanalytic Movement* (1916), and *Wit and Its Relation to the Unconscious* (1916), avant-garde American intellectuals had begun discussing the new psychology, which seemed to explain everything with theories of early sexual traumas, childhood fixations on mothers or fathers, repression of basic drives, and the transference of longings for desired objects to desires for obtainable, safe objects. In his Chicago Renaissance days, Anderson heard freethinking young artists discuss Freudian theory and practice analyzing one another. In middle age, Anderson may have been interested in the exciting new psychology so adoringly adopted by his cohorts, but in his writings he relied on commonsense observation and sensitive interpretation of actual human behavior, distilled and presented with art.[27]

Thus, in the years after its publication, *Winesburg, Ohio* could have been intelligently discussed as part of the revolt against the village, as literary naturalism, or as Freudian fiction. But for the rest of Anderson's life (he died in 1941), the stories actually received little discussion beyond simple admiration or simple detestation. Part of the problem was that Anderson was forty-two when *Winesburg, Ohio* appeared, and in his later writings he never quite measured up to his accomplishment in the Ohio stories. In the early 1920s Anderson was considered one of the eminent American writers, based on the stories in *Winesburg, Ohio,* in *The Triumph of the Egg,* and in *Horses and Men;* but he felt compelled to publish novels and wished to publish poetry and impressionistic essays, and never equaled his accomplishment in *Winesburg, Ohio* in any of his later collections of stories.

Still, younger writers were intrigued that Anderson had abandoned business for literature and by his brilliant demonstration of technique and subject matter in *Winesburg, Ohio* and later stories. He became in his lifetime an influence on Hemingway, Wolfe, Jean Toomer, Faulkner, K. A. Porter, Steinbeck, Welty, and other writers who were making their reputations while his own faltered. And it is because of the importance of his "pupils" in the 1950s and afterward that the reputation of Sherwood Anderson has been refurbished and reestablished, for when Hemingway and Faulkner and Steinbeck won Nobel Prizes for literature, American readers began to study seriously their beginnings—and at their beginnings was Sherwood Anderson, who may never rank *with* them but who must rank *near* them in literary importance.

In the last quarter-century, many studies have been published about Anderson and his Winesburg stories. Scholars have seen his work as an influence on Toomer's *Cane* (1923), Hemingway's *In Our Time* (1925), Steinbeck's *The Long Valley* (1938) and *Pastures of Heaven* (1932), Porter's Miranda stories, Faulkner's *Go Down, Moses* (1942), and Welty's *Golden Apples* (1949)—all story cycles comparable to and probably inspired by *Winesburg, Ohio.* There have been studies of *Winesburg, Ohio's* relation to other village stories, to other seemingly naturalistic stories, and to the whole body of twentieth-century fiction whose base is in Freudian and Jungian psychology. Recent studies have been done on Anderson's women characters in a time of female repression and on his wonderfully suggestive and consciously crafted prose. Yet the final word has not been written on these or any other aspects of *Winesburg, Ohio,* and the opportunity for original study and discovery awaits anyone who would read Anderson's story cycle sympathetically and diligently.

A READING

4

"The Book of the Grotesque"

Not until decades after *Winesburg, Ohio* was published in 1919 did scholars learn that Sherwood Anderson's intended title for the book had been *The Book of the Grotesque*. So accustomed are readers, critics, and historians to the title *Winesburg, Ohio* that any belated attempt to retitle the work would be futile and misleading. Still, recognition of Anderson's original title could aid greatly in understanding what the author was attempting in his book.

One further circumstance should be noted: on the contents page of the book (called "The Tales and the Persons") the first material listed is "The Book of the Grotesque." It is presented in print design as if it were the first of the *Winesburg, Ohio* tales. But "The Book of the Grotesque" is not a story; it is rather a mystical, oblique introduction to the stories that follow it, a fable of character and creation. Anderson published "The Book of the Grotesque" in a little magazine just before he published "Hands"—the first Winesburg story that Anderson composed—and he may have conceived "The Book of the Grotesque" separately from the stories about Winesburg and then realized that the earlier fable would be the appropriate introduction to his volume of stories.

For in "The Book of the Grotesque" there is no mention of the town

of Winesburg, Ohio, nor of any of the characters in the tales. There is instead the story of a man, a writer, "an old man with a white mustache"
(21), who hires an aging carpenter to build a platform for raising the bed
in his little room so that each morning he can look out freshly upon the
trees. (Anderson had such a raised bed in his Cass Street roominghouse in
Chicago.) But when they meet, instead of discussing the platform, the
two men smoke cigars and talk of other things. The carpenter tells the
writer pitifully about his brother, who died of starvation in a southern
prison camp during the Civil War. The platform is built later by the carpenter, but the old writer lies in bed, thinking of his mortality and his full
life and recalling people whom he has known, for "he had known people,
many people, known them in a peculiarly intimate way that was different
from the way in which you and I know people" (22).

Lying in bed between wakefulness and sleep and thinking of the
people he has known thus intimately in his life, the writer sees, "in a
dream that was not a dream" (22), passing in procession before him a vision of face after face. This unusual psychological phenomenon occasionally happened to Anderson himself, who described in private letters
and diaries just such processions of unusual characters passing before his
eyes in the darkness of his "nights of faces," as he called his half-asleep vi-
sions. The people who pass in procession before the eyes of the fictitious
old writer in "The Book of the Grotesque" are people whom he has
known but who have become somehow "grotesque": "All of the men and
women the writer had ever known had become grotesques" (22). After
seeing this procession in his bedroom for an hour, the old writer leaves
his bed to write of one of the faces that he has seen.

There is no certainty where Anderson found the word *grotesque* to
describe the figures in the mind of the old writer; perhaps the word came
from Edgar Allan Poe's 1840 *Tales of the Grotesque and Arabesque*, or
perhaps from discussions about art among Anderson's Chicago Renaissance friends. The word originated historically as the term for unlearned
drawings found on stone walls in Italian caves or grottoes—hence, to artists "grotesques" are drawings quickly limned, physically distorting, unlovely, and conjoining sometimes incongruous subjects.

Regardless of where Anderson found the word, it became for the old writer and for Anderson himself the operative locution for characters who have been bent, twisted, and pounded by life into often physically malformed creations. These characters are always psychologically distinctive and, to the sympathetic reader, are liable to be highly interesting.

Anderson pretends in "The Book of the Grotesque" to have actually seen the old writer's manuscript about the nighttime faces—unpublished tales collected under the title *The Book of the Grotesque*. But such an old writer and unpublished manuscript never existed except in Anderson's mind. He wrote of the controlling concept of the imagined book thus: "The book had one central thought that is very strange and has always remained with me. By remembering it I have been able to understand many people and things that I was never able to understand before.

> That in the beginning when the world was young there were a great many thoughts but no such thing as a truth. Man made the truths himself and each truth was a composite of a great many vague thoughts. All about in the world were the truths and they were all beautiful.
>
> The old man had listed hundreds of the truths in his book. I will not try to tell you of all of them. There was the truth of virginity and the truth of passion, the truth of wealth and of poverty, of thrift and of profligacy, of [carefulness] and abandon. Hundreds and hundreds were the truths and they were all beautiful. (23)

Anderson continues with his theory of human character in the guise of the old writer's idea: various people, coming along, gather up truths, which had all been positive, beautiful, and valuable; and collecting and living solely by the truth or truths that they claim and accumulate, each of the persons "became a grotesque and the truth he embraced became a falsehood" (24).

Alleging to have seen hundreds of pages of descriptions of the grotesque yet beautiful characters limned by the old writer, Anderson ends this mystical introduction to *Winesburg, Ohio* with the statement that the old carpenter, a sentimental character, exists only to show that "he, like many of what are called very common people, became the nearest thing to what is understandable and lovable of all the grotesques in the writer's book" (24).

This fable of grotesquerie—its belief that, by living by and for only one truth or one value or one assumption, humans become grotesque—may account adequately for some of the simpler characters in *Winesburg, Ohio,* but it is futile to read and study the stories as directly explicable by reference to this mystical introduction. Still, "The Book of the Grotesque" certainly prepares the reader for Anderson's stories of the often unlovely, the unloving, and the unhappy inhabitants of an imaginary Ohio town—characters endearing and fascinating to whoever would pause to recognize the beauty in these hitherto neglected, shunned, and grotesque human beings.

5

The Town and the Time

The name of the town of "Winesburg, Ohio" is so firmly established in the popular mind that it is often used in conjunction with "Main Street," "Peyton Place," "Zenith," "Harper Valley," and other fictional American locales as an image of a town that is replete with loneliness, repression, restriction, and only occasional rebellion and liberation. The easy use of "Winesburg, Ohio" to communicate such a cluster of implications of un-happiness is unfortunate, for such use conceals the true meaning of Anderson's book (although it does indicate that the book remains firmly a part of American culture). The subtitle of the book—*A Group of Tales of Ohio Small Town Life*—indicates that it is necessary to search at some length and in some depth for an understanding of the geography and the sociology of this important American literary town.

First, the reader should ignore the fact that in Ohio there actually is a town named Winesburg. Had Sherwood Anderson known or re-membered the existence of the real town in his native state, he would surely have chosen some other name for his fictive setting. The citizens of the real Winesburg, Ohio—in Holmes County, between Millersburg and Canton—were understandably not amused at their fair town seem-ingly becoming a direct model for a place of scandalous and shocking behavior; years after Anderson's book appeared, a minister in the real town wrote the author to complain of the confusion of the imaginary and the actual Winesburg. In reply, Anderson, who never saw the real Winesburg, apologized to the citizens through their minister for any implied insult and suggested that, if the citizens there were as wonderful and interesting as the citizens in the imaginary town, the real Winesburg, Ohio, had surely to be a very fine place.

Not Winesburg but Clyde, Ohio, was the model for Anderson's fictional town. The Anderson family had lived in Clyde from 1884 until after the mother's death in 1895; Sherwood left the town in 1895 or soon thereafter and seldom returned even to visit. He had bittersweet memories of a youth there of some poverty, much overwork, and alleged emotional starvation.

Clyde, which lies in the northern part of Ohio, in Green Creek Township in Sandusky County, had over three thousand citizens in 1895. It is located along the east-to-west Maumee and Western Reserve Turnpike, where it crossed two railroad lines, so the town enjoyed frequent train service. The east-west lines were the Lake Shore and the Wheeling and Lake Erie railroads, and the northeast-southwest line was the Indiana, Bloomington and Western Railroad. Clyde lies seventy-four miles from Cleveland, seventeen miles from both Tiffin and Sandusky, thirty-eight miles from Toledo, seven miles from Bellevue, and eight miles from Fremont, the seat of county government.

Near the crossing of the railroads in Anderson's day were two hotels, one of which was the Empire House. Scattered along the thirty-nine named streets of the town were various small churches—Methodist Episcopal, Regular Baptist, Presbyterian, Grace Protestant Episcopal, United Brethren, Lutheran, Universalist, St. Mary's Catholic, and Seventh Day Adventist. The dependable railroad service and the rich farmland of the area made Clyde an agricultural-service community and a valuable commercial source of vegetables, berries, apples, wheat, corn, oats, and hay. The town had an "opera house" for dramatic and musical presentations; a municipal waterworks pond; a racetrack and fairground; and a bicycle factory, in which Anderson worked briefly before he left town to make his fortune in Chicago, 282 miles to the west.

In 1919, after an older Sherwood Anderson had created the twenty-one stories that make up *Winesburg, Ohio,* the author and his publisher agreed that the book would be enhanced by a prefatory map of the imaginary town. To create a suitable map, Anderson supplied to Harald Toksvig, the Danish brother-in-law of writer and book reviewer Francis Hackett, a sketch from which Toksvig created an interesting "Map of Winesburg, Ohio," to be published inside the front covers of the first printings. The little map, drawn freehand by Toksvig, shows a railroad station beside an unnamed north-south railroad; Buckeye Street, running northward; Main Street, running westward; and approximately thirty houses and small business buildings scattered along these streets. Eight locales are identified in the legend on the Toksvig map: the office of the *Winesburg Eagle,* Hern's grocery, Sinnings' hardware, Biff Carter's Lunch Room, the railroad station, the New Willard House Hotel, the Fair Grounds, and the Waterworks Pond.

The mapped fictional Winesburg is starker and simpler than Clyde, Ohio—and far too small for eighteen hundred citizens. Yet it suggests schematically the layout of the real town of Anderson's youth. So far did Anderson go in using his hometown to establish Winesburg as a believable American town, worthy of study and exploration, that after 1919, the inevitable rumor sprang up that the actual citizens of Clyde and the actual circumstances and events in their lives had provided the models for the more grotesque characters in *Winesburg, Ohio.* One inhabitant even claimed to have a copy of the book in which the author wrote the names of the models for his creations in the margins. But the existence of such an annotated book seems unlikely, and any claim that Anderson directly copied from the citizens' lives seems unsubstantiated. Anderson's recreation of Clyde, Ohio, as Winesburg, Ohio, remains more geographical than autobiographical.

Exploring the fictional Winesburg is complicated by the fact that nowhere in the Winesburg stories—nor anywhere else—does Anderson lay out forthrightly the geography and the sociology of the town. The observing reader of *Winesburg, Ohio* must therefore scrupulously collect from Anderson's text all the scattered hints and implications about these vital matters, then organize them into the collage of a real if imaginary village.

Let us begin with geography. The imaginary village of Winesburg lies in North Central Ohio, eighteen miles south of the real town of Sandusky, which is on Lake Erie. The village of Winesburg is named after Wine Creek, a small stream that flows through the great basin of rolling hills surrounding the village. In the 1830s, twelve to fifteen houses standing around a general store constituted Winesburg, Ohio. Its location made it ripe to become a minor shipping point for an east-west railroad, to transport travelers and agricultural produce to and from the area.

Near the junction of Wine Creek and Trunion Pike, the village of Winesburg grew until, by the 1890s—the presumed time of the Winesburg stories—the population had swollen to eighteen hundred citizens. The farming areas surrounding the village had added several hundred residents to the county, an Ohio county that Anderson never bothers to name. Certainly, Winesburg is not important enough to be the seat of the imaginary county; and whatever town the county seat is, it is distinguished, to the people of Winesburg, by having the area's courthouse, along with a house of prostitution.

Groves of trees, many beech and maple trees and clumps of elders, still lie along streams near Winesburg in the 1890s. Long meadows surround Wine Creek. The town, centered in this pastoral scene, has kept maple and elm trees to shelter its major thoroughfares, which are Main Street, Maumee Street, Duane Street, Elm Street, and Buckeye Street. Some of these streets have been recently paved, and some are now edged with boardwalks. Minor, unpaved streets, unnamed by Anderson, lie adjacent to and are lined with cheap frame houses where day laborers live. Behind most of these poor houses are privies, kitchen gardens, pigsties, cowsheds, horse barns, and, near some of the older streets, the old Winesburg Cemetery, presumably filled with the town's peaceful dead.

The well-to-do people of Winesburg live in substantial homes, some built of brick or sandstone. They have stables for their horses and extensive yards with fine old trees that have thoughtfully been left to grow. Only the downtown commercial area is lighted at night, with natural gas. Where houses have been torn down or not yet built along the outlying streets, vacant lots are planted with corn and berries. Outside town, across cornfields and near wooded hills, lie the town's Waterworks Pond and, even farther out, the Fair Grounds, used for baseball games, autumn fairs, and occasional horse races.

The imaginary town can thus be reconstructed from widely scattered references to these and other common midwestern details of geography and history. Anderson also strews references throughout the book that indicate a full network of social institutions that would support a midwestern town of eighteen hundred people in the 1890s. There are two banking institutions—the Winesburg Savings Bank, John Hardy, President; and the Winesburg National Bank (also called the First National Bank of Winesburg), in which Elizabeth Swift and other citizens deposit their money and in which Henry Carpenter neatly keeps the books. Of professionals in Winesburg, there are four physicians, one retired lawyer, and several church ministers. Old Rufus Whiting still putters about his law office on Duane Street but solicits no new business. Of the several ministers, only the Reverend Curtis Hartman, of the proud Presbyterian Church of Winesburg, is named, although a Methodist Church is mentioned at least once in Anderson's stories. Of the four physicians, one is never named or described; the second, Doctor Parcival, may not be a real physician, after all, and anyway, he despises and avoids patients; the third, Doctor Welling, has an office on Main Street; and the fourth, Doctor Reefy, also the village dentist, survives nicely with present human-kindliness and the memory of one perfect love.

The town of Winesburg is served by the Big Four Railroad, which has a station and platform near the main hotel with a grassy area in front, surrounded by an iron railing; by the Western Union Telegraph Office, the dirtiest telegraph office in the entire state of Ohio; and by the United States Post Office, where works the laconic clerk Gertrude Wilmot. The town itself owns the Town Hall and may manage the Opera House (which is mentioned only once and apparently seldom used); the Winesburg Baseball Club, which wins games because its enthusiastic amateur coach confuses the opposing teams; a board of education that operates the Winesburg High School (no mention of any elementary school); and the Winesburg County Fair, with its horsetrack and decaying bleachers out of town, beyond Gospel Hill and Waterworks Pond, source of the village's water and ice supplies.

Several commercial establishments serve Winesburg's eighteen hundred citizens and the surrounding farm area. Abner Groff's bakery has a sullen owner who is in a glowering rage at life. Biff Carter's Lunch Room serves greasy leftovers as readily as fresh cooking. Cal Prouse's Barber Shop employs Art Wilson, apprentice barber and terror and blessing, he says, to the prostitutes in the county seat; Comstock's Mill grinds corn into meal. Cowley & Son's store has everything and sells little; Daugherty's Feed Store is undescribed; Ed Griffith's Saloon has an amorous if inarticulate bartender, Ed Handby. At Hern's grocery, coffee beans are fragrantly ground on Friday for the town's heavy Saturday custom; Herrick's Clothing Store places its discarded display equipment near Doctor Reefy's office door. At the millinery shop run by Mrs. Kate McHugh, the sensuous Belle Carpenter trims hats; Myerbaum's Notion Store is apparently a five-and-dime operation; the New Willard House (one of the most often-mentioned institutions in town) is fast approaching decrepitude. Above the Paris Dry Goods Company's Store, Doctor Reefy keeps his unventilated office; Sinnings' Hardware Store greatly outsells the rival Cowley & Son's. At Ransom Surbeck's pool room, young men meet to invent or recount and brag about sexual conquests. Sylvester West's Drug Store stays open late at night and sells cigars on demand to conquering young males. From the office of the Standard Oil Company, the industrious Joe Welling sells kerosene. Tom Willy's Saloon is as popular as Ed Griffith's Saloon in this town. Voight's wagon shop is located past Cowley & Son's, on Maumee Street; Wacker's Cigar Store is in competition with the drugstore tobacco dealers. Wesley Moyer's livery barn rents teams and rigs to all comers and boards horses for the well-to-do; Winney's Dry Goods Store makes two clothing stores for the village. The weekly newspaper is the *Winesburg Eagle,* the most often-mentioned business in Winesburg because young George Willard is the most frequently appearing character in Anderson's stories as the star and lone reporter there. He rushes about town to find and write up news items for the paper, which is published each Thursday morning.

Unnamed but clearly useful businesses include a carriage-painting shop; a horse-harness repair shop; a shoe repair shop; a feed barn and hay scale; a cider mill; a jewelry store; and a bookstore. This last establishment is probably not thriving, as it is mentioned only once in all of Anderson's pages. One small factory building remains vacant, the barrel-stave business that was originally there having closed. Not described but possibly extant in a village of eighteen hundred people in the mid–1890s and definitely needed are a blacksmith, a veterinarian, a produce buyer, a teamster or carter, a dealer in land, and an undertaker (although undertakers are sure also to be found in that unnamed county seat, along with those noted prostitutes).

Anderson did not consciously set out, when inventing this town, to create a background of photographic verisimilitude that chronicled every one of the inhabitants of Winesburg and the outlying countryside. But it is remarkable how broadly and naturally Anderson does casually populate this town. Leaving out characters invented merely to give the major characters a family connection or a motivation, Anderson's background painting provides an entire panoply of village characters, from Jerry Bird, the town drunk, who lies uncomfortably asleep in alleyways, to Banker White, who lies comfortably (and surely soberly) asleep in his new brick home on Elm Street. Named townsmen and townswomen have such occupations as butcher, housekeeper, vehicle merchant, store clerk, nurseryman, schoolteacher, express agent, baggageman, berry farmer, chicken farmer, serving girl, and of course, the old lamplighter of long, long ago.

Just as Anderson never provides in one place a full description of his imagined town, he nowhere provides a specific date in either the nineteenth or the twentieth century when the stories "happened." This makes it necessary to look at the overall chronological setting of Anderson's stories for the presumed date of present action.[28]

As a first clue, the author steps into the story cycle occasionally and refers to general times past. For example, in "An Awakening" he recalls: "In Winesburg, as in all Ohio towns of twenty years ago . . ." (184); and in "Godliness" he summarizes the great changes in American society since the Civil War: "In the last fifty years . . ." (70). In order to date the action of the Winesburg stories, the reader must remember that Anderson was writing the stories no earlier than late 1915 and no later than 1918, the time when he was living in Chicago. Thus, the narrative present—the time that Anderson uses for the present in the tales—should be between 1895 and 1898.

The reader should then notice the chronology of the four stories in which newspaper reporter George Willard plays no part at all or none beyond simple mention: "Godliness," "Adventure," "The Untold Lie," and "Paper Pills." The action in these four stories and in part of "Death" occurs before the narrative present of the rest of the stories, 1895–98.

The four-part "Godliness," by far the longest Winesburg story, is also the most historical and the most epochal. Jesse Bentley, a product of historical forces and individual religious fanaticism, is transformed by the Civil War from an eighteen-year-old seminary student into a twenty-two-year-old farmer. By twenty-three, Jesse is both a father and a widower. His daughter, Louise, at fifteen attends school in Winesburg. There she comes to love and seduces a young man. They marry, and he becomes the father of Jesse's grandson, David Hardy. Jesse, therefore, has to be fifty-two when twelve-year-old David comes to live at the Bentley farms. Jesse must be fifty-five but looks seventy when he stupidly causes the permanent disappearance of his beloved grandson from his life and from the area. Thus, the date of the final events in "Godliness" is no later than 1898.

In "The Untold Lie" Anderson has a slight problem with narrative perspective, for he originally published the story in a periodical with first-person narration; and in book form he retains evidence of the earlier form, saying that Winesburg is "our town" (203), making himself a boy when a character's father committed suicide. There is no way to date the autumn setting of this story more precisely, since it has nothing more to do with the recurring character George Willard.

In "Adventure," George Willard is referred to as "a mere boy" (112) when Alice Hindman, the main character of the story, is twenty-seven. Within the story, there are statements that Alice is abandoned by her lover at sixteen, loses her father to death at twenty-two, analyzes her serious loneliness at twenty-five, and suffers a sudden emotional trauma at twenty-seven, thereafter becoming resigned to a completely empty life. In frustration, she joins the Epworth League (117), a Methodist youth organization founded in 1889, so the story "Adventure" occurs in the early 1890s, when George Willard would indeed have been "a mere boy" of thirteen or fourteen.

In only one story, "Paper Pills," does Anderson seem to have difficulty with chronology, for the facts of the story simply do not fit comfortably into the overall chronology of *Winesburg, Ohio*. The marriage of Doctor Reefy to an unnamed young woman occurs when he is forty-five, and by the narrative present he has been living alone for ten years after her death. And in "Death," Doctor Reefy is described as being middle-aged (close to forty) when George Willard's ill mother, age forty-one, visits his office. Doctor Reefy next sees Elizabeth Willard when she is a corpse, at age forty-five. He is said to have then married an unnamed younger woman with whom he discussed the case of Elizabeth Willard in their one winter of happiness before the wife died. Logically, then, Doctor Reefy's narrative present has to be after 1895, when he comforts George Willard in the presence of the youth's dead mother and when he forms his brief marriage and begins his ten years of loneliness. This would mean that the action of *Winesburg, Ohio* extends into the twentieth century, perhaps to 1906—a result that Anderson surely did not intend.

Thus, the internal chronology of the stories of *Winesburg, Ohio* is for the most part believable and untroubling with the exception of the events in "Paper Pills" and "Death." Still, in *Winesburg, Ohio* there are surprisingly few topical references to events external to the fictional setting and the happenings Anderson created. In fact, only a reference to the friendship of William McKinley and Mark Hanna (132) relates the tales directly to the larger, real world; this friendship between Cleveland businessman Hanna and McKinley, the governor of Ohio (1891–95) and later U.S. president (1897–1901), a friendship that is assumed to be tainted with money and political favor, is mentioned by Anderson only once in passing as a subject being discussed loudly by the men of Winesburg.

Thus, the careful explorer of Winesburg, Ohio, will find that the fictional town is laid out with considerable geographical and sociological detail and that it is set in a chronology that in its internal consistency creates no serious problems.

6

The Youth

The reader of *Winesburg, Ohio* is apt to put the book down remembering especially well only one character—George Willard. George is the character most often met and, being a pleasant youth, the character with whom the reader perhaps most closely identifies.

The first thing that must be said about George Willard is that he is not Sherwood Anderson, in either fact or wish. For one thing, Anderson had many siblings and thought his family shamefully poor; George is an only child and enjoys a measure of respect and prosperity because his mother owns and his father operates the New Willard House, even if that hotel is becoming timeworn. As a youth Anderson helped support his family by selling newspapers on the streets of Clyde, Ohio; George is a reporter for the weekly *Winesburg Eagle*. Anderson scarcely attended high school in Clyde; George has recently graduated from Winesburg High School. As an adult, Anderson might have wished to believe that when young he had great ambition to become a successful writer; the young George definitely has the great ambition to become a successful writer. All that the two men share, all things considered, is residence in a small Ohio town in the late nineteenth century and the death of a mother that frees each to move from his small town into the great awaiting world.

Although George Willard is of minimal importance in four of the Winesburg stories, notice must be taken of exactly what he is and does in the remaining stories, both those in which he is secondary but nonetheless an active participant and is somehow affected, and those in which he is without question a principal character.

There are eleven Winesburg stories in which George Willard plays a secondary but important part: "Hands," "Mother," "The Philosopher," "A Man of Ideas," "Respectability," "The Thinker," "Tandy," "The Strength of God," "Loneliness," " 'Queer,' " and "Drink." Again, Anderson nowhere fully describes George Willard and his position in the life of the town, and it is therefore necessary to gather scattered information about the youth as Anderson presents it, bit by bit, from the facts and hints that accumulate throughout the story cycle. We will first learn what we can from the stories in which he is a secondary but still important character.

George Willard is first presented, in "Hands," as an occasional visitor to the small house of Wing Biddlebaum, on the edge of Winesburg. Only when he is with George Willard can Wing Biddlebaum walk boldly and confidently through the streets of the town near which he has lived for twenty years but in which he is otherwise fearful and timid. In "something like a friendship" (27) with George, Wing lets himself walk with the youth and lectures him movingly on topics that are dear to his heart and important for George to hear: "The voice that had been low and trembling became shrill and loud. The bent figure straightened. With a kind of wriggle, like a fish returned to the brook by the fisherman, Biddlebaum the silent began to talk, striving to put into words the ideas that had been accumulated by his mind during long years of silence" (28).

This frustrated little man, in his eagerness to teach his one unofficial pupil, one day lets his hands, ordinarily concealed, become active, expressive, and almost affectionate toward the youth. The older man notes the involuntary motions of his hands and runs panicked away from George and back to the safe obscurity of his little house. George, who had been on the verge of asking about the nervous and usually hidden hands, finds himself suddenly alone.

George will never ask about Wing's mysterious hands; he may never return to walk with and listen to the would-be teacher; and, saddest of all, being less than perceptive or well read, he has missed the point of Wing's recent talk: "Wing Biddlebaum made a picture for George Willard. In the picture men lived again in a kind of pastoral golden age. Across a green open country came clean-limbed young men, some afoot, some mounted upon horses. In crowds the young men came to gather about the feet of an old man who sat beneath a tree in a tiny garden and who talked to them" (30). George will probably never grasp that Wing was talking of Plato and his wonderful *Akademeia,* founded in a grove of trees in Athens in 387 B.C. Yet the young man may, after all, have heard the more direct advice of the frustrated and fearful friend and teacher: "You have the inclination to be alone and to dream and you are afraid of dreams. You want to be like others in town here. You hear them talk and you try to imitate them. . . . You must try to forget all you have learned. . . . You must begin to dream. From this time on you must shut your ears to the roaring of the voices" (30). As George will never ask about his older friend's hands, he may well never return to learn more of life; only time will reveal whether he has learned from Wing Biddlebaum to be himself, to question and listen to himself, and to dare to dream.

In "Mother," George is a subject of controversy—a seemingly unspoken and mutually unacknowledged controversy—between Elizabeth Willard and her husband, Tom. The father, always briskly efficient and full of bonhomie toward hotel guests and townspeople, dwells in disappointment that his good activities as a brave Democrat in a mostly Republican territory have not led him to political preferment; and the mother, always moping dejectedly around the hotel she owns, is keenly and dramatically frustrated by her unloving marriage and her lifelong entrapment in the constricting small town. Both parents would have their one child fulfill in his life their own unfulfilled ambitions.

In his room in the hotel, Tom Willard advises George about the proper course of conduct for the bright son of a clearly successful man.

Having used his influence to gain for the youth the position of reporter on the *Winesburg Eagle,* the father lectures George on proper gratitude and proper advancement through life. Citing complaints from Will Henderson, the newspaper publisher, about George's daydreaming and lack of responsiveness, the father concludes (after George's unreported defense): "Well, I guess you'll get over it. . . . I told Will that. You're not a fool and you're not a woman. You're Tom Willard's son and you'll wake up. I'm not afraid. What you say clears things up. If being a newspaper man had put the notion of becoming a writer into your mind that's all right. Only I guess you'll have to wake up to do that too, eh?" (44). Here the reader learns, for the first time in *Winesburg, Ohio,* that George has informed some of the townspeople and his father that he has chosen a profession—that he intends to be a writer. In this story, George is given a further bit of delineation—he talks pleasantly to himself when alone in his room—a practice that his mother overhears, giving her joy that the boy is "not a dull clod, all words and smartness" (43).

The third story in *Winesburg, Ohio* that involves George Willard in a secondary role is "The Philosopher." It concerns Doctor Parcival, one of the four town physicians, if he is indeed a physician, for he dislikes patients and spends his time trying to make himself matter to someone —in this case, to George. George has been reporting for the *Winesburg Eagle* for a year, and Doctor Parcival repeatedly seeks him out when Will Henderson is gone and the boy is alone in the newspaper office, for "the acquaintanceship was entirely a matter of the doctor's own making" (49). To George (and presumably to him alone in Winesburg), Parcival would teach "the advisability of adopting a line of conduct that he was himself unable to define" (50). He challenges the youth to be a real investigative reporter and to investigate, for example, the mystery surrounding Parcival himself. The doctor confesses: "I have a desire to make you admire me, that's a fact. I don't know why. That's why I talk. It's very amusing, eh?" (50). The youth is very easily drawn to the tales the doctor tells of himself: "He began to admire the fat unclean-looking man and, in the afternoon when Will Henderson had gone, looked forward with keen interest to the doctor's coming" (50).

Claiming to have been a small-town newspaper reporter in Illinois or in Iowa, Parcival suggests his possible involvement in the murder of a physician in Chicago; and he talks (perhaps truthfully) of his rivalry with his brother for their mother's affection and of his father's unfortunate death in an asylum. Stopping his tales suddenly one day, the doctor pours forth his philosophy: "I want to fill you with hatred and contempt so that you will be a superior being" (55). Once again, someone in Winesburg is trying to teach George a philosophy of life; this time, instead of the Platonist wisdom of Wing Biddlebaum, Doctor Parcival would teach the youth the Nietzschean idea of the superman, the supremely egoistic and therefore superior being. Captivated by the doctor's words if not by his ideas, for the next month George regularly visits Parcival in his office instead of waiting for him to come to the newspaper office. One afternoon, after an unfortunate accident in the streets of Winesburg, Doctor Parcival is in panic and terror of imminent death. He appoints George his disciple, his follower: "If something happens perhaps you will be able to write the book that I may never get written. The idea is very simple, so simple that if you are not careful you will forget it. It is this—that everyone in the world is Christ and they are all crucified. That's what I want to say. Don't you forget that. Whatever happens, don't you dare let yourself forget" (56–57). There is no evidence that George understands or grasps this seemingly profound philosophy, but in Doctor Parcival, his mind has been strongly challenged to comprehend an unexpectedly complex human character and one possibly dangerous in the seemingly bucolic town of Winesburg, Ohio.

George witnesses another event after reporting for the *Eagle* for a year, the instance, told of in "A Man of Ideas," of the occasionally strange behavior of Joe Welling. Welling is a successful local agent for the Standard Oil Company and, when he is under a manic spell of talking, an overwhelming force to unfortunate listeners. Still again, a citizen of Winesburg would teach George about being a good reporter. Joe suggests that George write in his reporter's notebook, for example, a monumental headline about the world being on fire—that is, about decay, representing the constant state of the world's burning, through oxidation. George fears, with the rest of the Winesburg citizenry, that Joe will be murdered by the gruesome father and the dangerous brother of the beloved and silent Sarah King. He observes in fascination that the fast-talking and seemingly intellectually alive Joe Welling remains ignorant of the present danger to himself by discoursing innocently and spontaneously about his newest discovery—the human race's amazing ability to reinvent vegetables should all the current crops ever be devastated. Here, in "A Man of Ideas," the observant youth finds no particular wisdom, unless it be the unstated supposition that, to a young man striving to become a writer, words are magical and wondrous things.

After the lighthearted fun of "A Man of Ideas" and whatever that experience may have held for George, the boy encounters, in another citizen of Winesburg, a serious and very somber view of life. In "Respectability," George is sought out by the physically filthy telegraph operator Wash Williams, who would warn him to abandon his evening walks with the lovely Belle Carpenter, a worker in the millinery shop of Mrs. Kate McHugh, and his possible fascination with her lush charms. To no one else in Winesburg does Wash Williams want to tell the cautionary story of his own life; but he proves so uncommunicative that George must start the conversation himself by suggesting that Williams was perhaps once married and that Mrs. Williams has died. To his amazement, there immediately pours from the telegraph operator a torrent of black oaths, curses upon all women, and malediction for all men so easily made fools of by women. The boy listens to the lesson "afire with curiosity" (124): "I tell you, all women are dead, my mother, your mother, that tall dark woman who works in the millinery store and with whom I saw you walking about yesterday—all of them, they are all dead. I tell you there is something rotten about them" (124). In the almost total darkness of night in which they sit, the rapt George feels that "there was something almost beautiful in the voice of Wash Williams, the hideous, telling his story of hate" (125). Although George begins listening to the telegraph operator's story "afire with curiosity," after he hears of the female deceit and wickedness practiced upon the once idealistic and now embittered telegraph operator, "the boy's body shook as from a chill" (127). Having received lessons in Platonism, Nietzschean idealism, the power of words, and profound misogyny, George Willard—whether already sadder or wiser is unclear—will face the remaining lessons that life in Winesburg, Ohio, can teach him.

George's role in "The Thinker," is only to inadvertently inspire his friend Seth Richmond, one of the quieter youths of the town, into making a gesture toward maturity. George has always sought out Seth to talk to, for being almost silent, Seth is wrongly assumed to be a profound thinker; George has been talking to him of becoming, after his years with the *Eagle*, a true writer. Now Seth comes at night to visit George in his room at the New Willard House. George smokes a manly pipe and announces that to learn to write well, he must try to write a story about love; and he says that Helen White, daughter of one of the town's bankers and a childhood friend of Seth's, will do just fine for the necessary experience. He asks Seth to convey to Helen the message that George loves her and to bring back to George a detailed account of the result of this prime announcement. Thereupon, George drops out of "The Thinker," for the story does not primarily concern him. His appearance here simply confirms that many in Winesburg know from George's bragging that he intends to become an author of important literature. But in this story his indirectly empirical attitude toward love marks George as still quite insensitive and emotionally unsophisticated.

"Tandy," a brief story approximately halfway through *Winesburg, Ohio,* is the least discussed of Sherwood Anderson's Ohio stories, probably because its meaning is unclear. Perhaps it is unfinished; perhaps it is a fable more about love than about any person; perhaps it was not originally written for *Winesburg, Ohio*. In this tale of a mysterious stranger who arrives from the wicked city to conquer his alcoholism in a wholesome small town, George Willard, as in "A Man of Ideas," views an almost prophetlike stranger and listens to the ostensibly important words that he speaks. His impressive words grandiloquently propose a theory of love in which the lover and the beloved are always unequal. The lover, he says, is always hunting for a woman strong enough to dare to be loved but does not find her among the world's women. The words spoken, he challenges a small listening girl to grow up to be "tandy"— the stranger's neologism for strongly loving. The stranger abandons Winesburg, leaving George to ponder what he has heard. Perhaps the philosophy of love here spoken has implications for the maturing young man; perhaps now, in contrast to his easy idea of love in "The Thinker," George will develop more respect for the difficulties of finding love in his life. Whatever it is, the message of "Tandy" remains obscure.

"The Strength of God" is a companion story to "The Teacher," in which George Willard is a major character; so George cannot be discussed in "The Strength of God" without some reference to the interlocking plot of "The Teacher." In January, the coldest month in Winesburg's winter, George Willard is sitting "in the office of the *Winesburg Eagle* trying to write a story" (153). From the bell tower of his church, the Reverend Curtis Hartman is peeping lustfully and at length into the next-door bedroom of Kate Swift, one of the village schoolteachers. Later that bitter night, the reverend bursts into the *Eagle* office to inform the already troubled youth: "I have found the light. . . . After ten years in this town, God has manifested himself to me in the body of a woman. . . . God has appeared to me in the person of Kate Swift, the school teacher, kneeling naked on a bed. . . . Although she may not be aware of it, she is an instrument of God, bearing the message of truth" (155). His declaration made, the minister raises his bleeding fist, declaring that, with the strength of God, he has destroyed a window, which must now be replaced. Earlier that same night, in the very newspaper office into which the Reverend Hartman has precipitately burst, George has had his own personal difficulties with Kate Swift, related in "The Teacher." There is no clear message for the youth in "The Strength of God," only a certain increase in his wonderment at the confusion and the ineffability of life—and his inability yet (if ever) to comprehend any sure meanings from life.

George has a clearer role (if not clearer understanding) in "Loneliness," the next story that concerns him as a secondary character. In October, a sad time of the year for romantic souls of any age, when nature becomes barren and the sensitive walk wet streets alone at night, George is invited to visit the room of Enoch Robinson, a native of Winesburg who was for many years a resident among artists in New York City: "The boy was a little afraid but had never been more curious in his life. A hundred times he had heard the old man spoken of as a little off his head and he thought himself rather brave and manly to go at all" (174–75). In long hours of talk, Enoch tells George his piteous tale of childlike innocence and anger among the adults in the great city. He ends his narration with a description of the destruction of his city dreams and says: "Don't stay here with me any more. I thought it might be a good thing to tell you but it isn't. I don't want to talk any more. Go away" (177). But the young listener forcefully commands: "Don't stop now. Tell me the rest of it. . . . What happened? Tell me the rest of the story" (177). Sadly no more of Enoch Robinson's dream life remains to be told in response to the youth's imperious command. As George leaves the older man's once-safe sanctuary in Winesburg, he hears behind him his "whimpering and complaining. 'I'm alone, all alone here. . . . It was warm and friendly in my room but now I'm all alone' " (178). George is likely unaware of the damage that he has done—for by learning of the would-be artist's only companions, the friends of his imagination, he has destroyed them. The young man then walks away from one of the more pathetic and endearing grotesques of *Winesburg, Ohio.* Is he wiser? Probably not.

In two more of the stories George Willard also plays secondary but important roles—" 'Queer' " and "Drink." In the first of these stories, Elmer Cowley, against his will, has been moved from the more rural and peaceful area of the county by his ex-farmer businessman father. As George goes briskly about the town collecting information for his newspaper, he seems to be accepted by and to belong among the regular people of Winesburg, and he becomes to the unsophisticated Elmer Cowley a hated and resented object. George represents to the disoriented, isolated, and anxious Elmer the censure of the town; "Did he not represent public opinion and had not the public opinion of Winesburg condemned the Cowleys to queerness? Did he not walk whistling and laughing through Main Street? Might not one by striking his person strike also the greater enemy—the thing that smiled and went its own way—the judgment of Winesburg?" (194). At midnight, before he boards a freight train bound for some huge city where he hopes (futilely, of course) to better fit into society, Elmer Cowley beats George half-unconscious on the station platform, leaving the reporter doubtless amazed at the sudden violence from one whom he had considered at most a possibly interesting fellow.

If Elmer Cowley could never, despite his best efforts, feel part of the town of Winesburg, in "Drink" Tom Foster, too, has been moved to Winesburg from elsewhere—in Tom's case, from the more unwholesome areas of the city of Cincinnati, areas of "ugliness and crime and lust" (215). But Tom Foster, a youth, fits immediately and smoothly into the life of Winesburg, where he is an uncomplicated and regular young fellow. Still inwardly Tom, like Elmer, comes to feel remote from real life, disconnected emotionally from everyone. He creates for himself a love object whom he can win imaginatively, while he is thoroughly drunk. Tom thinks romantically of Helen White, daughter of one of the town's bankers and by now also something of a romantic interest to George. Tom confesses drunkenly to George as if his imagined love scene with Helen were a reality. Afterward, Tom sobers enough to explain to George that he needs to be drunk in order to feel, for the first time in years, at all emotional about something or someone. But "George Willard did not see, but his anger concerning Helen White passed and he felt drawn toward the pale, shaken boy as he had never before been drawn toward anyone" (218). Motherly and solicitous as he may be with Tom, George is ignorant of Tom's motive and simply cannot understand any such need for suffering, for feeling. Again, George Willard comes up against his psychological limitations.

In these eleven stories, George Willard is not an especially strong or attractive character as he goes about his personal errands and his professional duties in Winesburg, Ohio. But in the five stories in Anderson's cycle in which George is a major character, he emerges more clearly as a cardinal protagonist and unifies Anderson's short fictions into the equivalent of a traditional bildungsroman, a novel of initiation.

"Nobody Knows," the fifth of the twenty-one Winesburg stories, finds George nervously ready for a sexual adventure, presumably the loss of his original sexual innocence. He has received a wonderful note from one of the town's more appealing and more available young women, Louise Trunnion: "I'm yours if you want me" (60). Waiting until night can cover his guilty actions, George pulls his concealing hat down over his face and makes secretive progress through the back alleys of the town. He avoids the townspeople, who somehow manage to go about shopping and visiting, totally unaware of the momentous adventure on which the youth is bound—his quest for the emotional intimacy and the hard adult knowledge of sexual congress. The aggressive Louise Trunnion has probably sought him out because of his social position and his obvious innocence, but this warm night, George, despite his strong drive for sexual activity, must deliberately force himself to continue on his quest: "He did not dare think. In his mind there was a fear but it was a new kind of fear. He was afraid the adventure on which he had set out would be spoiled, that he would lose courage and turn back" (59). He finds Louise cleaning in her father's cottage in the poorer part of Winesburg and is totally confused by her initial comment—"You think you're better than I am. Don't tell me, I guess I know" (60). Unexpectedly, George has to convince the woman who so boldly offered herself to him in her note. Now near his goal, he "became wholly the male, bold and aggressive. In his heart there was no sympathy for her" (61). And he must argue, " 'Ah, come on, it'll be all right. There won't be anyone know anything. How can they know?' he urged" (61).

Anderson placed ellipses at this point in the text, revealing absolutely nothing more about Louise's physical conquest of George. The little remaining narrative of "Nobody Knows" concerns only the initiated youth, for no word is said about tenderness, gratitude, or concern for the woman. There is not even a hint that George accompanies the woman back to her poor house. Instead, the youth is next met when his adventure is over and he is already returning, walking boldly down the very Main Street this time, back to the comfortable context of his ordinary life. Wanting somehow to talk (but surely not to brag) to some man, any man, the youth buys a cigar and chats innocuously with the drugstore clerk, Shorty Crandall, about adult matters of some sort. Then, continuing alone toward home, some fear gives him pause, and George mutters to himself: "She hasn't got anything on me. Nobody knows" (62). And indeed, no one but Louise Trunnion will ever know about the sexual initiation granted to the youthful newspaper reporter. Sadly, after his necessary expedition into carnal experience is over, not a great deal is after all different in his life. But George can now, without regret, with only mild guilt, and with little fear of the woman claiming his male freedom, get on with the remainder of his life. Nobody knows—nobody knows what?

George Willard is not a protagonist in another *Winesburg, Ohio* story until "The Teacher," the thirteenth story, which concerns the newspaper reporter and Kate Swift, a high school teacher. "The Teacher" is a well-narrated story, for the author recreates one whole day in the life of George Willard, from his Thursday-morning walk into the countryside to think until his last waking moments in bed late that night. George has taken the day off from work. Again, the problem George faces is sexual: he worries—or perhaps he hopes—that his former high school English teacher is somehow attracted to him or even in love with him.

On his walk, George considers the evidence that the usually emotionally frigid Kate is attracted to him. In his latest talks with her about his desire to be a writer, he has not understood all of what she has tried to teach him. Last summer, Kate took him to the deserted Fair Grounds for a lecture about writing, and ever since, he has been puzzling in his somewhat slow way over her advice: "It would be better to give up the notion of writing until you are better prepared. Now it's time to be living. I don't want to frighten you, but I would like to make you understand the import of what you think of attempting. You must not become a mere peddler of words. The thing to learn is to know what people are thinking about, not what they say" (163). On the previous evening, he went to Kate's home to borrow a book from her. She kissed him lightly and, both of them embarrassed, had said harshly: "What's the use? It will be ten years before you begin to understand what I mean when I talk to you" (164).

George returns from his countryside ramble, and in the afternoon he lies in his warm bed at the family hotel and thinks sexual, perhaps masturbatory thoughts, first of Kate (a forbidden subject) and then of Helen White, daughter of a local banker (a safe subject), "with whom he had been for a long time half in love" (158). After a comforting afternoon sleep, George spends Thursday evening in the newspaper office, busy at his writing. He is visited there by the lonely English teacher, who has been warmly attracted to the glow of light in the office window on this bitterly cold night—and to her maturing ex-student, George Willard. Again Kate lectures him, and again she concludes: "I must be going. . . . In a moment, if I stay, I'll be wanting to kiss you" (164). And into his strong arms the young man does take the agitated woman. Perhaps he is ready to play the part of a man and love her physically; but she beats sharply with her fists on his face and runs from the office, leaving George "swearing furiously" (165)—probably at his own timidity or cowardice in letting her escape from fulfillment of their mutual physical need. Into this scene of mad frustration comes the Reverend Curtis Hartman, the seemingly demented Presbyterian minister, announcing with a bleeding fist that God has appeared to him in the form of Kate Swift and that he has smashed the entire window. The baffled George ends his day lying in his bed again, now icy-cold, and thinking: "I have missed something Kate Swift was trying to tell me" (166). Clearly, George Willard is not yet sufficiently aware of human needs and vulnerabilities to be, for good or ill, a typical, conquering young male.

George Willard has one more sexual adventure in *Winesburg, Ohio*, this one in "An Awakening." The story concerns Belle Carpenter, the headstrong and handsome trimmer of hats in a local millinery—the very woman against whose wiles Wash Williams, the unwashed telegraph operator, has so eloquently warned the boy in "Respectability." Belle is in love with the strong but nonverbal Ed Handby, a local bartender, but she walks evenings with George Willard "as a kind of relief to her feelings" (180). For the evening of what will be their last walk, George has worked himself into a very romantic mood. Joining in the man-talk of the youths at Ransom Surbeck's pool room, George announced "that women should look out for themselves, that the fellow who went out with a girl was not responsible for what happened" (182). He has walked almost transcendentally through the back streets of town, imagining himself first a leader of soldiers, able to make them orderly and to bring order into his own life; second, a resident of a fragrant medieval town; and third, a detached observer of ordinary life in his own small town. Overcome with emotion, elated with himself, and ready to say the great words "Death. . . night, the sea, fear, loveliness" (185), George is ready to share his high excitement with a woman—and Belle Carpenter will do nicely as the woman.

He walks at length with the attractive Belle, trying to impress her with talk of his new-felt manliness. He follows Belle up a hill, where, he is sure, he will make love to her. But Ed Handby, the jealous suitor for Belle, is following them. George embraces Belle and, still in the mood for enormous words, announces, "Lust . . . lust and night and women" (188), only to be flung aside three times by the attacking bartender, who is ready to valiantly march his woman home. Unlike the conclusion of "Nobody Knows," George Willard creeps, humiliated, back toward his own part of Winesburg, finding the poor streets, so recently energizing, "utterly squalid and commonplace" (189).

George Willard has no more sexual adventures comparable to his successful quest in "Nobody Knows" or to his failing mission in "An Awakening." But the young man has two more Winesburg stories in which to play a leading part; and in one, George is well paired with a young woman—finally, the suitable and very attractive Helen White, who has grown up with George in Winesburg but who has for some time been away from their hometown to attend a women's college.

One autumn day when Winesburg is enjoying its county fair, George Willard, at eighteen, feels detached from the crowds in the town streets and the people talking loudly of their personal and business affairs. He wishes he were with Helen White, instead, but her mother has invited a pompous young male instructor from the college to visit Winesburg for the holiday. George, hoping to leave town soon to work on some city newspaper, has been feeling different lately: "He felt old and a little tired. Memories awoke in him. To his mind his new sense of maturity set him apart, made of him a half-tragic figure. He wanted someone to understand the feeling that had taken possession of him after his mother's death" (234).

Helen White, having been away for study, has also been feeling different lately: "She was no longer a girl and hungered to reach into the grace and beauty of womanhood" (235); and "she thought that the months she had spent in the city, the going to theaters and the seeing of great crowds wandering in lighted thoroughfares, had changed her profoundly. She wanted him to feel and be conscious of the change in her nature" (236). Tonight, both George and Helen, some little distance apart, are remembering their time together the past summer, when he boastfully declared his plan to become important in life; he remembers his trust in her and his hope that she would be a beautiful woman.

Now, each finds the other ready to be together quietly, away from the crowds and noise of Winesburg. This autumn evening, the two silently walk to the Fair Ground, where they sit silently, kissing but once, holding tight to each other and both silently thinking: "I have come to this lonely place and here is this other" (241). In all of *Winesburg, Ohio* there is no closer bonding possible than this quiet acceptance and trust between George and Helen, between two people who silently recognize each other's individuality and integrity. This is true maturity, true sophistication; and "man or boy, woman or girl, they had for a moment taken hold of the thing that makes the mature life of men and women in the modern world possible" (243).

Even though they are complete with each other in this one fine moment of understanding, there is no assertion or even hint that George and Helen are destined to advance easily and happily with each other into love and marriage. No such optimistic ending to *Winesburg, Ohio* would be credible or acceptable; and Anderson carefully ends the cycle of stories with "Departure," in which, the following spring, young George leaves his hometown for work in a great city. Anderson does not say which city; the connecting railroad could take him to either New York

City or Chicago—anyway, out of his midwestern town. His memories play over in the departing young man's mind: but it is typical village scenes that come to him, not his moment of love with Helen White or the emotionally charged encounters with Wing Biddlebaum, Doctor Parcival, Enoch Robinson, Kate Swift, or the other grotesque characters whose lives have touched his own. The reader is thus left unaware of the impact that the experiences with deeper life that he has endured or enjoyed in Winesburg, Ohio, has had on the maturing George Willard. He is, when last seen, apparently just another ordinary Ohio youth leaving his small hometown for the greater world.

And yet in the last paragraph of "Departure," Anderson does allow the reader one last glimpse into George's inner world. When George's mind is "carried away by his growing passion for dreams" (247), Winesburg has for him "disappeared and his life there had become but a background on which to paint the dreams of his manhood" (247). There is no assurance whatever that his future holds greatness as a writer or even as a human being; and yet there is here some hope that the first and most important advice this youth has been given—that of Wing Biddlebaum in "Hands," to dare to dream and to listen to his dreams— has been understood and incorporated.

The reader may sense a problem in reading this story cycle as a novel of initiation: that George Willard as the initiated hero and the maturing protagonist of *Winesburg, Ohio* is unimpressive. Perhaps that problem results from the presentation of the stories in an imperfect chronological order, and perhaps a study of the stories in a more traditional chronological order will clear up the reader's unease with the disappointing leading character.

The major action of "Hands," the first-drafted Winesburg story, clearly occurs some time before the other stories. It is tempting to think that the remaining Winesburg stories appear in chronological order. Sixteen of the twenty remaining stories seem to do so. In such a simple scheme, each of these sixteen stories corresponds to a month or season in the narrative present:

The Youth

1. "Mother"—July
2. "The Philosopher"—August
3. "Nobody Knows"—August/September
4. "A Man Of Ideas"—May
5. "Respectability"—Summer
6. "The Thinker"—June
7. "Tandy"—Summer
8. "The Strength of God"—January
9. "The Teacher"—January
10. "Loneliness"—October
11. "An Awakening"—January
12. " 'Queer' "—November
13. "Drink"—Spring
14. "Death"—March
15. "Sophistication"—Fall
16. "Departure"—April

Such an ordering by season or month can carry the reader through George Willard's development in Winesburg, Ohio, and his departure at age nineteen. But this chronology still leaves unsettled which episodes happen just when, the age of the central character at the time of certain events, the time of his birthday, and whether the sixteen stories cover one, two, or three years.

A study of George Willard in chronological order should begin in July of his first year of reporting for the *Winesburg Eagle*. Elizabeth Willard is forty-five in "Mother"—the same age she is in "Death," which takes place many months after her son's quiet announcement that he will eventually leave Winesburg. According to "Death," Elizabeth was forty-one when she and Doctor Reefy almost made love and when George was a boy of twelve or fourteen. Therefore, at least four years pass before Elizabeth Willard dies at forty-five on a Friday in March of the year when her son is eighteen.

If George begins reporting for the *Eagle* soon after his graduation from high school, as seems likely, he must be seventeen years old during this first summer of newspaper work. Perhaps his experiences in "Hands" and "Mother" occur that summer, as well as his first known sexual encounter in "Nobody Knows." If he last visits Wing Biddlebaum in

"Hands" in May or June and if he talks with his neurotic mother in July about his future departure, his next adventure is later that same summer, in August or September, when on a night that is warm and cloudy, he and Louise Trunnion have sex in a berry field in "Nobody Knows."

This order violates the presentation of Anderson's narrative-present stories as published in 1919. In "The Philosopher" and in "A Man of Ideas," George has worked for the *Eagle* for a year when Doctor Parcival intrigues him with misanthropy and Christlike suffering, and when Joe Welling becomes a New Willard House resident, manages the baseball team, and falls in love with Sarah King. These two episodes should happen, then, when George is eighteen, one year and some weeks after he completes high school and becomes a newspaper reporter. Presumably the stranger's prophecy in "Tandy," too, occurs in George's first summer of work on the *Eagle*; and his summer of initiation into sex in "Nobody Knows" incorporates his walking about town with the sensuous Belle Carpenter in "An Awakening." These frustrating walks should take place in George's seventeenth summer, for in spite of Wash Williams's dire warnings in "Respectability," the youth continues to foolishly be used by Belle Carpenter until "An Awakening" comes to him on a cold night the following January. One further story should occur in the autumn of George Willard's seventeenth year— "Loneliness," in which George shares an adolescent melancholy with the much-older Enoch Robinson.

Thus, "Mother," "Nobody Knows," "Respectability," "Tandy," and "Loneliness" should all happen in the summer and autumn of George Willard's seventeenth year—the first year of action in the narrative present of the stories—conjecturally, 1894. Because George is eighteen when his mother dies in March and is still eighteen the following autumn, his birthday must fall during winter, perhaps in January, so that he is nineteen at his final appearance, in "Departure." Since "Departure" is the only Winesburg story that occurs in the third year of narrative present— presumably in 1896—ten of Anderson's stories must occur in 1895—the eighteenth and most important year in George Willard's life.

This ten-story group should begin with "An Awakening," which is definitely set in January (even though to romantic, transcendent George the night air is sweet and fresh—a perfect deceptive setting for Belle Carpenter's pretended seduction of the youth). Supposedly in the same month, on the coldest, darkest night of the year, the Reverend Curtis Hartman peeps secretly at Kate Swift from the ice-cold bell tower of the Presbyterian Church; and Kate Swift—in Winesburg "the most eagerly passionate soul among them" (162) —almost dares to seduce George near the roaring fire in the office of the *Winesburg Eagle*.

In March, at three o'clock on a Friday afternoon, Elizabeth Willard in "Death" finds her last lover after lying paralyzed for several days, mutely unable to give to her son either encouragement or the hoard of money treasured by her and that could have been his escape from the deadening town. Only slowly does George realize his mother is dead that day; and only thirteen months later does he fulfill his mother's dream by departing from the confinements of Winesburg.

"Drink" should occur next, in the spring of 1895, George's eighteenth year, for Tom Foster undergoes his solitary, drunken reentry into emotional life in the spring. He is eighteen, but still somewhat younger than George. George's tenure on the *Eagle* reaches one year, and in May of the summer of his eighteenth year, he is amazed by the inadvertent but pragmatically effective oratory of Joe Welling in "A Man of Ideas." In August he is momentarily dazzled by the misanthropic would-be martyrdom of Doctor Parcival in "The Philosopher." In June, between the Joe Welling and Doctor Parcival episodes, must come "The Thinker," for at eighteen the silent and superficial Seth Richmond, somewhat younger than George, tries unsuccessfully to court Helen White in jealous response to George's interest in her.

In the autumn of 1895, George shares his moment of maturity—his unspoken mutual acceptance—with Helen White. On the evening of the last day of the annual county fair, George is lonely and preparing to leave Winesburg; Helen White has already gone away, perhaps to Cleveland, to attend college. In "Sophistication," George recalls his braggart behavior when he was with Helen the previous summer, his eighteenth. Now he is maturing—in contrast to Elmer Cowley, who, in " 'Queer,' " envies George's new overcoat and his presumed place of prominence in the town. In November, when Elmer impulsively leaves Winesburg to chase the phantasm of the normal, George quietly and confidently plans his own departure from the town the coming spring.

Having turned nineteen in the winter of 1895–96, in April 1896—thirteen months after his mother's death in March of his eighteenth year and twenty-one months after his declaration of intent to depart in "Mother"—George boards the westbound train from Cleveland, which will take him to another railroad crossing, where he will board another train for either New York City or Chicago. In one of those cities—away from Winesburg, yet forever with the town in his mind—George may begin painting on the canvas of his youth in Winesburg, Ohio, the continuing "dreams of his manhood" (247).

SCHEMATIC CHRONOLOGY FOR *WINESBURG, OHIO*

Narrative Past

1. "Godliness"
2. "The Untold Lie"
3. "Adventure"
4. "Paper Pills" and part of "Death"
5. "Hands"

Narrative Present

1894

1. "Mother"—July
2. "Nobody Knows"—August/September
3. "Respectability"—Summer
4. "Tandy"—Summer
5. "Loneliness"—Autumn

1895

1. "An Awakening"—January
2. "The Strength of God"—January
3. "The Teacher"—January
4. "Death"—March
5. "Drink"—Spring
6. "A Man of Ideas"—May

7. "The Thinker"—June
8. "The Philosopher"—August
9. "Sophistication"—September/October
10. " 'Queer' "—November

1896

"Departure"

Having studied the *Winesburg, Ohio* stories either in the sequence in which Anderson presented them in 1919 or as rearranged artificially to make George Willard's growth and initiation the controlling pattern of the cycle, the thoughtful reader may believe George to be a well-developed, well-rounded character, who carries the burden of meaning in the stories. But some of the grotesque characters of *Winesburg, Ohio* come into contact with George and some of them are unaware of his presence near their lives. The thoughtful reader may therefore prefer to consider this story cycle as something more than an interesting study of the initiation into experience of a typical young American midwesterner.

7

The Grotesques

Sherwood Anderson's *Winesburg, Ohio* presents an interesting description and dramatization of a typical midwestern American town in the 1890s, complete with the citizens and the institutions associated with such places. It can also be read pleasurably as the description and dramatization of a youth's initiation or growing toward adult understanding in a typical midwestern American town in the 1890s. But neither of these approaches sufficiently explains the greatness of Anderson's achievement in *Winesburg, Ohio*—why readers since 1919 have read the book with a new sense of the power of writing. For Anderson captures in words the most elusive and the most buried of human impulses and motivations; in short, he fulfills the aim of his dedication of his book to his mother, Emma Smith Anderson, "whose keen observations on the life about her first awoke in me the hunger to see beneath the surface of lives." It is through Anderson's understanding and expression of the buried aspects of human character that he reaches genius in *Winesburg, Ohio*.

In the first of the *Winesburg, Ohio* stories, "Hands," Anderson brings the reader near the town but not actually into the town. Wing

Biddlebaum, the central character, has lived near the town for twenty years but has not in any sense been a part of it. His decaying little house sits in a field near a ravine and away from the road to town, so Wing must look across a field that is planted to clover but that bears only mustard weeds to see even ordinary life passing him by.

Nicknamed for the continuing nervous movements of his hands (which in season can pick amazing amounts of berries), Wing has told and will tell no one his secret: that he, born Adolph Myers, was for years a public schoolteacher in Pennsylvania; that he was accused of misusing his hands; and that he was driven from the area instead of being hanged, as the townspeople had first planned. The reader must accept Anderson's statement that Wing Biddlebaum is so innocent that he has never comprehended and can never comprehend the nature of the accusation against him. His behavior as a teacher is described thus: "With the boys of his school, Adolph Myers had walked in the evening or had sat talking until dusk upon the schoolhouse steps lost in a kind of dream. Here and there went his hands, caressing the shoulders of the boys, playing about the tousled heads. As he talked his voice became soft and musical. There was a caress in that also. In a way the voice and the hands, the stroking of the shoulders and the touching of the hair were a part of the schoolmaster's effort to carry a dream into the young minds" (31).

In the Pennsylvania school, a retarded pupil had dreamed of sexual activities with the innocent schoolmaster and had recounted his completely imagined actions as if they had really happened. The teacher was expelled from his community and from his lifework. After fleeing to Ohio, Myers has lived near Winesburg as Wing Biddlebaum ever since, alone in "a ghostly band of doubts" (27), with neither friend nor companion. Recently, George Willard has become curious and has occasionally come to walk with the little man—not, certainly, as the possible source of a newspaper story but as the source of an interesting acquaintanceship.

Here in the first Winesburg story, Anderson uses a narrative technique that is also found in the best of the twenty remaining stories: a physical peculiarity hints to the reader the presence of a psychological peculiarity. The unusually active hands of Wing Biddlebaum lead the reader to awareness that one of the few intellectuals in *Winesburg, Ohio* has an unusual mental and psychological constitution. The hands "became his distinguishing feature, the source of his fame. Also they made more grotesque an already grotesque and elusive individuality" (29). Wing is not physically crippled by his hand movements, nor is he intellectually crippled by what has happened to him. Yet he is emotionally crippled, eternally frozen and fearful by the inexplicable (to him) events of twenty years ago. He is endowed with the love and motivation necessary to be a great teacher, but untrue, hysterical accusations based on community misunderstanding of the erotic dreams of a retardate have victimized him.

To present-day sophisticates in matters of sexual desire and frustration, Wing's complete ignorance of the "horrors" of which he was accused those long years ago may seem implausible. But the reader must simply accept this character as a completely Platonic personality, unable to conceive of the crimes of which he was accused—which were, of course, homosexuality and pedophilia. Self-ignorance and public stupidity have destroyed the good that Wing Biddlebaum could have given to a world already starved for intellect and inspiration. His life, intended by nature for growing clover, has produced instead only dense and useless mustard weeds.

If the reader is ready to suspect that unhappiness and frustration come to Anderson's grotesque characters merely because they are cursed with living in or near Winesburg, attention should be paid to the fact that Wing's terrible trauma—his emotionally crippling event—happened twenty years ago in Pennsylvania. Not all agony and grotesquerie come from Winesburg, Ohio.

If "Hands" brings the reader close—geographically and thematically —to the town of Winesburg, "Paper Pills," the second Winesburg story, is the most inviting introduction to the element of the grotesque in the Winesburg stories. The story concerns the sudden, brief, and enigmatic marriage of an older doctor and one of his younger patients. Anderson compares the richness and texture of their story to some of the fruit of the apple trees that grow near Winesburg:

It is delicious, like the twisted little apples that grow in the orchards of Winesburg. In the fall one walks in the orchards and the ground is hard with frost underfoot. The apples have been taken from the trees by the pickers. . . . On the trees are only a few gnarled apples that the pickers have rejected. They look like the knuckles of Doctor Reefy's hands. One nibbles at them and they are delicious. Into a little round place at the side of the apple has been gathered all of its sweetness. One runs from tree to tree over the frosted ground picking the gnarled, twisted apples and filling his pockets with them. Only the few know the sweetness of the twisted apples. (36)

Similarly, the sensitive and perceptive reader will understand the unexpected attraction, the sweetness, of the manifestly twisted human personalities in *Winesburg, Ohio.*

"Paper Pills" is the story of Doctor Reefy, the most competent and likable of Winesburg's four physicians. Anderson presents him as one who is coping adequately with what life has dealt him: his loneliness. Years ago, he had married a tall, dark girl, who is never named, but the following spring, he suddenly lost her to an unspecified disease. Ever since her death, the doctor has worn the same articles of clothing; he has sat, usually alone, in his drab and musty office; he has tried only once— and failed—to open the window of that office to the outside air and light; and he has in those years alone been unsentimentally friendly with only one person, John Spaniard, the Winesburg nurseryman.

Doctor Reefy, with his grotesquely malformed knuckles, has a peculiar habit: he writes down upon pieces of paper his "thoughts, ends of thoughts, beginnings of thoughts" (37). He stuffs these fragments of paper continually into his pockets, so that eventually the particles of thoughts become hardened into little round balls—the "paper pills" of Anderson's title: "he worked ceaselessly, building up something that he himself destroyed. Little pyramids of truth he erected and after erecting knocked them down again that he might have the truths to erect other pyramids" (35).

Doctor Reefy is the true philosopher of Winesburg, Ohio—the person who has faced the problem of evil, of life's unfairness and injustices. Despite his manifold unspecified and discarded thoughts, he has achieved no unified theory to explain the vagaries and meaninglessness of human existence. From his thoughts the doctor "formed a truth that arose gigantic in his mind. The truth clouded the world. It became terrible and then faded away and the little thoughts began again" (37). Thus, "Paper Pills" demonstrates Anderson's typical use of grotesquerie: a character, somewhat physically unusual, is hurt deeply by life, ponders over his state of anomie, and realizes that there are no gods to whom to pray but nevertheless copes with the grayness that is life for him.

The most interesting grotesque of "Paper Pills" is not Doctor Reefy but the unnamed young woman to whom he so briefly and happily was married. In telling her story, Anderson uses concepts from psychology—here, the importance of dreaming and emotional displacement. When the young woman's parents died, she inherited considerable wealth. She was courted by several young men, typified by two: "a slender young man with white hands, the son of a jeweler in Winesburg, [who] talked continually of virginity" (37), and "a black-haired boy with large ears, [who] said nothing at all but always managed to get her into the darkness, where he began to kiss her" (37). The young woman, properly fearful of the pale, virginity-obsessed youth, comes to see that "beneath his talk of virginity . . . there was a lust greater than in all the others" (37). In her three dreams about this youth, she imagines him holding, turning, and staring at her body; and three times "she dreamed that he had bitten into her body and that his jaws were dripping" (37).

Surely in unconscious fear of the pale and dangerous suitor, the woman lets the dark and silent suitor seduce her (and in the seduction bite her shoulder). Subconsciously threatened by one suitor and actually bitten and impregnated by the other, she comes, motherless, to Doctor Reefy for childbearing advice. First, she sees him in his office, efficiently and kindly pulling the teeth of a suffering woman. Then the miracle: in some aspect of Doctor Reefy, bearer of huge, gnarled knuckles, perhaps in his gentleness as healer of pain and wounds, this young woman, hurt and "bitten" in life, "discovered the sweetness of the twisted apples"; and "she could not get her mind fixed again upon the round perfect fruit" (38). The two characters immediately fall in love and in the autumn marry, to the amazement and confusion of the townspeople. During their few months together, the doctor "read to her all of the odds and ends of thoughts he had scribbled on the bits of paper" (38). She loses her un-born (and to the doctor, unimportant) child and dies in the spring of an unspecified disease. Since then, Doctor Reefy has continued to sit alone and to write his thoughts about life upon scraps of paper, thoughts that come—necessarily and inevitably—to nothing.

Because Elizabeth Willard is the central character in two of the Winesburg stories, "Mother" and "Death," she is one of the more fully realized of the grotesques in Anderson's stories. The reader learns a great deal about this frustrated woman, from her unhappy youth, spent with-out a mother to guide her, to her happier demise, at only forty-five, and the personification of death as a handsome gentleman-caller who comes to greet and escort her.

In "Mother" (a title that makes Elizabeth Willard represent certain universal qualities of motherhood), the reader learns of a crisis in the wom-an's life. She must defend her son, George, from the influence of her hus-band, Tom, who would have the boy learn mainly to win friends and influence people on the road to social and financial success. Like Wing Biddlebaum and Doctor Reefy, Elizabeth exhibits a slight physical gro-tesquerie—facial smallpox scars. She is always listless and exhausted: "Al-though she was but forty-five, some obscure disease had taken the fire out of her figure" (39), making her a "tall ghostly figure, moving slowly through the halls" (39) of her hotel. But this woman's grotesquerie is more clearly psychological than physical—her inability to fulfill her girlhood dreams of escape or to directly commission her son George to achieve his own escape and happiness. For although the boy and the mother sympa-thize with each other, they cannot express their communion or sympathy verbally. She has forgotten how to communicate, and he has never learned to speak forthrightly to his silent and suffering mother.

In "Mother," the imagery used to describe Elizabeth Willard's life involves an easy identification of her with a mistreated cat that she sees through her bedroom window. In this seeming "picture of village life" (41), the gray cat, belonging to the druggist, Sylvester West, competes with Winesburg baker Abner Groff for the bread of life. The cat steals food to survive, and the baker, in an enormous rage, tries to hit and kill the cat. So closely and personally does Elizabeth Willard identify with this cat that "once when she was alone, and after watching a prolonged and ineffectual outburst on the part of the baker, Elizabeth Willard put her head down on her long white hands and wept" (41). The scene of struggle "seemed like a rehearsal of her own life, terrible in its vividness" (41).

Imagery from the theater—the melodramatic "scene" between cat and baker, the repeated brutal "rehearsal" of the woman's life—continues, when Anderson describes the youthful and rebellious Elizabeth Willard as having been an unhappy adolescent, a frustrated actress, who wished to escape from the town of Winesburg with the troupes of traveling actors who passed through her father's hotel, thinking that away, somewhere, elsewhere, she could be happy. In her frustration and boredom, she became an easy conquest for traveling actors and other men and found it emotionally gratifying, but she wondered why completing the sex act did not affect the worldly men as romantically as it repeatedly affected her.

Theatrical imagery continues further when the ill, aging woman is called upon to dramatically defend her son from his father. She will paint her face with old theatrical makeup to render herself once more beautiful; and she will "act," play out a histrionic scene in the lobby of the hotel. She will defend young George from Tom's vicious influence by stabbing her hated husband to death and then somehow herself dying: "As a tigress whose cub had been threatened would she appear, coming out of the shadows, stealing noiselessly along and holding the long wicked scissors in her hand" (47).

In *Winesburg, Ohio*, the great scenes that are planned are seldom successfully played out as scripted. And so it is that Elizabeth Willard, at the end of "Mother," sits in her room in weakness and darkness. When her son suddenly appears to announce quietly his eventual departure from the town, something she has longed to do herself for so long, she is, as usual, unable to voice her total approval and delight and can only recast her husband's overheard advice about George being smart and successful. Although Elizabeth is now assured that George will in time leave

Winesburg, he will do so not of her direct urging. Her imagined theatrical scene of murder and vengeance will never be performed, and this sad woman will remain alone with her delusions and her thwarted ambitions.

In "Mother," Anderson uses in the word "adventure" for the first time in *Winesburg, Ohio* (42)—a term that he thereafter uses frequently to indicate that a character has come to the one brief moment, the one epiphany, the one telling instant, that captures and communicates the essence of that character's personality, leaving nothing more to be said or learned about him or her. When Elizabeth Willard, worried that she has not been visited by George for several days, overhears Tom's practical advice to him about getting ahead, she must then prepare for and execute her one "adventure"—her just and murderous release of both her son and herself from the hold of Winesburg, Ohio. Often in Anderson's stories the described "adventure" is the first and presumably the only time that a character realizes how frustrated he or she is and therefore tries to take strong measures—usually unsuccessfully—toward satisfaction, rebellion, or self-completion.

"Death," written after Anderson completed most of the other Winesburg stories, adds detail and pathos to Elizabeth Willard's unhappy story, including loss of her mother when she was five. Here Anderson applies the word "adventure" five times to her lifelong quest for love. Elizabeth recalls "her girlhood with its passionate longing for *adventure* and she remembered the arms of men that had held her when *adventure* was a possible thing for her" (222–23). "In her girlhood and young womanhood," he narrates, "Elizabeth had tried to be a real *adventurer* in life" (224); in her youthful affairs with various men, "she had never entered upon an *adventure* prompted by desire alone" (224); and "in all the babble of words that fell from the lips of the men with whom she *adventured* she was trying to find what would be for her the true word" (224).

Anderson also changes the operative metaphor for Elizabeth's frustration and longing, replacing the theatrical, feline imagery of "Mother" with the more traditional imagery of circumvented romantic love. Here Anderson recounts her one-time almost-lovemaking with Doctor Reefy.

For her, at forty-one, the episode is the closest to happy acceptance and understanding that she will experience. Having repeatedly contemplated her approaching death as the ultimate patient wait for her beautiful male lover, she declines in health and dies on a Friday in March in the afternoon (Christlike?). She was mute for a month from paralysis, unable to tell her beloved son George of the money, hidden in the wall of her bedroom, that she has kept ever since her youth to effect her own and now, she hopes, his escape from Winesburg.

The last words spoken over the gaunt and tired corpse of Elizabeth Willard reveal Anderson's belief that even in the most unlovely and grotesque human beings the observant witness can find a bit of secret sweetness hidden in the "twisted apples." With Elizabeth lying dead in her hotel room, her son in his grief finally understands the essence of her life and says: "The dear, the dear, oh the lovely dear" (232). He does not know that four years earlier, in a moment of understanding, Doctor Reefy had thought of the unhappy woman visiting his office and muttered, "You dear! You lovely dear! Oh you lovely dear!" (227). In turn, Doctor Reefy did not know that one of the numerous men with whom Elizabeth had adventured in her youth "in the moment of his passion had cried out to her more than a hundred times, saying the same words madly over and over: 'You dear! You dear! You lovely dear!'" (223).

In contrast to the useful and well-coping Doctor Reefy is Anderson's next grotesque character, the misanthropic and explosive Doctor Parcival. He, too, has a measure of physical grotesquerie: "His teeth were black and irregular and there was something strange about his eyes. The lid of the left eye twitched; it fell down and snapped up" (49). This perhaps self-proclaimed physician has arrived mysteriously in Winesburg and has lived there mysteriously. He mysteriously seeks out George Willard to anoint as his disciple in misanthropy. The psychological grotesquerie of Doctor Parcival is easy to diagnose: he has suffered from an inferiority complex since childhood, having been reared by a mother who loved his less-civilized brother better and having failed to become a Presbyterian minister. He has taken no good care of himself physically, socially, or professionally in Winesburg. This masochist, in reaction to his deep inferiority complex, preaches to George Willard a doctrine of individual primacy, challenging the youth to become superior to common people.

This unhappy man has his "adventure" (55) one day in August, when George visits his office to hear more of the doctrine of superiority. When the doctor is summoned to aid a young girl who has been struck down by horses in the street, the physician refuses to go. For this man, refusing to give medical help in an emergency is a deliberate act of cruelty, and he predicts that his arrogant refusal will bring the enraged townspeople to hang him by the neck from a lamppost on Main Street. This does not in fact occur because the doctor's refusal—like his self-importance—has not been noticed by Winesburg's citizens. Frustrated for now in his "adventure," his sought-after martyrdom, his attempt to matter to people, his expected crucifixion nonetheless will, he asserts, sometime surely come. Doctor Parcival commissions George to write a book based on his philosophy, that "everyone in the world is Christ and they are all crucified. That's what I want to say. Don't you forget that. Whatever happens, don't you dare let yourself forget" (57). There is, alas, no evidence that Doctor Parcival, his self-predicted martyrdom—comparing himself to the most famous martyr in history—or his quite absurd if wonderful-sounding philosophy has impressed George Willard, or anyone else in the world.

Anderson might have originally conceived the four-part story "Godliness" as a novel; it covers the most pages and the most time of all the Winesburg stories. It recounts the growth of agricultural industrialization in the Midwest and one man's religious fanaticism and its effects on his daughter and grandson. Locating "Godliness" in American history is easy, for the central turning point is the Civil War and its effects on the Bentley family, who live on a farm outside Winesburg.

Jesse Bentley's brothers died in the Civil War, and his father subsequently retreated from responsibility. Intended for a career as a Presbyterian minister, Jesse, the weakest of the Bentley sons, leaves his seminary studies to operate the family farm. Uninformed about traditional agriculture, he is willing to try new, perhaps scientific ways of producing crops in the unpromising fields. Jesse brings from the city a wife, Katherine, who is however unlikely to survive a life of hard labor on a northern Ohio farm before mechanization: "Jesse was hard with her as he was with everybody about him in those days. She tried to do such work as all the neighbor women about her did and he let her go on without interference" (67). This maltreated wife becomes the first victim of the harsh treatment and fanatic dedication of Jesse Bentley.

Wealth is not Jesse's sole object. As he becomes successful in farming, he tries to unite his fundamentalist Presbyterian religious beliefs with his robust financial drive. Believing in the Old Testament doctrine of a "covenant" or bargain between God and the righteous man, Jesse comes to see himself as God's agent in an unrighteous world. "Look upon me, O God," he prays, "and look Thou also upon my neighbors and all the men who have gone before me here! O God, create in me another Jesse, like that one of old, to rule over men and to be the father of sons who shall be rulers!" (70). He derives his beliefs from the Old Testament, with its emphasis on the covenant, rather than from the New Testament, with its emphasis on love, and seeks the direct commission from God that the covenant implies. He desires to found a dynasty near Winesburg, Ohio: "It seemed to him that in his day as in those other and older days, kingdoms might be created and new impulses given to the lives of men by the power of God speaking through a chosen servant. He longed to be such a servant" (70). The Bentley dynasty is to begin with the birth of Jesse's first child, a son, to be named David: "Jehovah of Hosts . . . send to me this night out of the womb of Katherine, a son. Let Thy grace alight upon me. Send me a son to be called David who shall help me to pluck at last all of these lands out of the hands of the Philistines and turn them to Thy service and to the building of Thy kingdom on earth" (73).

But the child born to Jesse and Katherine Bentley is a girl, and Katherine dies in childbirth. The fanatic's desire to found an invincible dynasty is frustrated. He resents his undesired female offspring, and the child, Louise Bentley, finds little love or joy in her isolated farm environment. The father, prospering still and expanding his farm, sends her to board with the Hardy family in Winesburg in order to attend school. Here the unloved and resented Louise Bentley has her own "adventure" (92), the occasion that forms and fixes her behavior for the rest of her life.

Feeling cut off as if by a wall (one of Anderson's recurring images of human anomie) from all other people, including her cold, religious father, Louise is yet eager to belong among others. This rich but naïve farm girl secretly witnesses a scene of lovemaking between one of the Hardy women and a lover. Wanting desperately to be cherished by someone, Louise writes a note to John Hardy, the son: "I want someone to love me and I want to love someone" (94). He responds, and afterward, fearful that Louise has become pregnant, John Hardy and Louise Bentley marry. But the fear of pregnancy proves false. The two are nevertheless married —a situation not promising for the endurance of young love. To them is eventually born one child, a son named David, who in his turn grows up in maternal lovelessness and resentment. "It is a man child and will get what it wants," Louise thinks. "Had it been a woman child there is nothing in the world I would not have done for it" (96). David Hardy is the victim of his mother's ill-nature and hatred, just as Louise herself is victim of Jesse's ill-nature and neglect.

In the narration of "Godliness," Anderson commits several infelicities; perhaps, if the story began as a novel, he had to reshape it into a brief *Winesburg, Ohio* story but kept some of the freedom that is allowed in longer narrative but inappropriate in the short-story form. For example, in the third part of "Godliness," called "Surrender," he describes Louise Bentley Hardy as "from childhood a neurotic, one of the race of over-sensitive women that in later days industrialism was to bring in such great numbers into the world" (87). How much better Anderson does when he merely describes unusual behavior instead of diagnosing it with a medical term such as "neurotic." In the four parts of this story of three generations of Bentleys and Hardys, he too often reaches for historical breadth, lecturing the reader on the nature of industrialism and its dehumanizing influence upon American people. Put simply, in "Godliness," as in the other Winesburg tales, Anderson should show instead of tell.

Yet there are moments of satisfying narration in "Godliness," as when young David Hardy, troubled or threatened by fears, simply turns his face and hides his eyes from the world; as when Louise Bentley, first wanting love from a human, tries to seduce but merely unnerves a farm-hand; as when David runs away from home for the first time, and Louise treats him for once with proper maternal love and becomes to him literally a different (and perhaps disconcerting) woman; as when David moves permanently to the Bentley farm to live and the entire Bentley household becomes a sunny and comforting place.

When David comes to live with his grandfather, he becomes the male heir and vehicle through which Jesse will try to establish his godly dynasty in the valley of Wine Creek. Jesse finds himself with the beloved youth in a wood one day soon after. Jesse, feeling again in tune with God and confident of his rewards for the faithful, goes through a ceremony among the trees that invokes a sign from God: "Into the old man's mind had come the notion that now he could bring from God a word or a sign out of the sky, that the presence of the boy and man on their knees in some lonely spot in the forest would make the miracle he had been waiting for almost inevitable" (85). Jesse, too, now finally has a symptom of physical grotesquerie—"he had been threatened with paralysis and his left side remained somewhat weakened. As he talked his left eyelid twitched" (81)—and as he fervently prays to his God, the old man holds David and shouts to the sky: "Here I stand with the boy David. Come down to me out of the sky and make Thy presence known to me" (86). So frightened is David that he cries out against "a terrible man back there in the woods" (86); the grandfather, ignoring the degree of his grandson's terror, simply thinks that his God does not yet approve of him.

Later, when he is fifteen, David Hardy is once again frightened in his grandfather's wood, and this occurrence is the boy's "adventure" (97) as well as his final appearance in *Winesburg, Ohio*. Having received from his God a most bounteous harvest on his many farms, Jesse Bentley decides in the autumn that a complete biblical ceremony of thanksgiving is in order. He takes with him his grandson and a newborn lamb so that he can reenact the Old Testament ritual of sacrifice. The old man in his intensity so terrifies the boy that David runs away from the frightening fanatic and shoots a stone with his slingshot. Thinking that he has killed the evil, terrifying figure, he concludes: "I have killed the man of God and now I will myself be a man and go into the world" (102). David is never heard from again. The fanatical old Jesse, when questioned, mutters only: "It happened because I was too greedy for glory" (102). Thus the curse of the Bentleys is carried from generation unto generation. Jesse Bentley's conviction that he must become a prophet of the God of the Bible makes him one of the more easily diagnosed grotesques in *Winesburg, Ohio,* one of those who have seized upon a truth and, living by that single truth, have become grotesque while that truth becomes a lie.

Not all the characters in *Winesburg, Ohio* are grotesque. Some of the townspeople, grotesque only occasionally, are capable of functioning quite well in their careers and in the life of their community. Such a reasonably well-adjusted person is Joe Welling in "A Man of Ideas." Son of "a grey, silent woman with a peculiarly ashy complexion" (103) and a now-deceased man of some political prominence, Joe (the usual "Joe" of the world) is briskly efficient at selling products for the Standard Oil Company and goes about daily life. Only now and then does he trouble his neighbors with fits of unstoppable talking. Because the ideas he expresses in his "logorrhea" are true but unimportant (life is burning up, oxidizing; rain has fallen recently in a neighboring county), the town's citizens are wary of this "tiny little volcano that lies silent for days and then suddenly spouts fire" (103), this occasional oracle with gold-tipped teeth (his physical grotesquerie?) who will surely marry the uncolorful Sarah King, a woman as ashy and silent as Joe's mother.

Midway through *Winesburg, Ohio* and immediately after the attempted light humor of "A Man of Ideas" comes "Adventure," one of the best narrated and most completely realized stories of the grotesque. George Willard is of no importance in this story, and little external or topical matter is involved in its plot, so "Adventure" is the best single "separable" story of the cycle to illustrate of the author's subject matter and technique.

There is little physical grotesquerie in "Adventure." Alice Hindman's one unusual feature is that her head "was large and overshadowed her body" (112); and as she aged, "her shoulders were a little stooped and her hair and eyes brown. She was very quiet but beneath a placid exterior a continual ferment went on" (112). This ordinary-seeming woman, as Anderson masterfully constructs her, exemplifies his theory that the buried life is the best subject matter for fiction. For Alice Hindman's emotional life is buried deeply beneath the placid surface that she presents to the world everyday as she clerks efficiently in Winney's Dry Goods Store, becoming pensive and brooding only on rainy days, when there are few customers to attend, and when she must turn inward for matter to contemplate.

In "Adventure," the reader learns of the events of eleven years of Alice Hindman's life, from age sixteen until the moment of her present "adventure" at age twenty-seven, when her life becomes forever set, desperate, and hopeless. No great trauma begins this woman's secret despair; when she is sixteen, simply "betrayed by her desire to have something beautiful come into her rather narrow life" (112), Alice becomes physically intimate with Ned Currie, a predecessor of George Willard on the staff of the *Winesburg Eagle*. Their courtship is interesting, for Alice, at sixteen, is quite liberated for her time. She states her desire to accompany Ned, unmarried, to Cleveland so that he can advance his career as a newspaperman there while she works to help support them: "I do not want to harness you to a needless expense that will prevent your making progress. Don't marry me now. We will get along without that and we can be together. Even though we live in the same house no one will say anything. In the city we will be unknown and people will pay no attention to us" (113). Confronted with a young woman confident of her own mind in their affair and willing to love him on equal terms, Ned, in typical male fashion, immediately reverses his emotional direction. From wanting Alice to become his mistress, he now wants her to become the passive object of his love who waits patiently at home while he goes off to heroically earn enough money to support her as he desires. Ned promises to return for her when he has sufficient funds for their wedding and married life together, and he makes love to her on the evening before his departure from Winesburg: "It did not seem to them that anything that could happen in the future could blot out the wonder and beauty of the thing that had happened. 'Now we will have to stick to each other, whatever happens we will have to do that,' Ned Currie said as he left the girl at her father's door" (113–14). Of course, as the reader expects, Ned forgets about Alice as soon as he moves from Cleveland to distant Chicago, where his new friends make his life urbanely interesting and exciting.

"Adventure" is the story of Alice Hindman left behind, alone in Winesburg. Anderson describes three points in her loneliness to demonstrate the development of her extreme isolation. By twenty-two, six years after being left alone, Alice has lost her father to death, seen her mother become a carpet weaver, and begun to clerk at Winney's. As money was the problem six years ago, she saves the money she earns, "thinking that when she had saved two or three hundred dollars she would follow her lover to the city and try if her presence would not win back his affections" (114). She resists friendships offered by other young Winesburg adults and looks only backward upon her one quick adolescent affair. She "felt that she could never marry another man. To her the thought of giving to another what she still felt could belong only to Ned seemed monstrous" (114–15). Thus, working and saving for a "purpose" and yet surely aware of her abandonment as eternal, not temporary, Alice "began to practice the devices common to lonely people" (115). She prays at night in her upstairs bedroom, but her words are intended not for her God but for her lover. She becomes possessive about the very furniture in her room, forbidding anyone else to touch it, since she can have and hold tangible objects, as she surely cannot have and hold Ned. The money she earns at her job, she pretends, will become abundant enough to generate sufficient interest income to support her husband and herself; she remembers in particular, and surely not ironically, Ned Currie's love of travel. Continually she whispers, weeping to herself: "Oh, Ned, I am waiting" (116).

Alice, growing older and lonelier in her little Ohio town, is given, for better or worse, a gift of self-understanding not vouchsafed to most of the grotesque characters in *Winesburg, Ohio.* She is frequently overwhelmed by a "fear of age and ineffectuality" (116); she "realized that for her the beauty and freshness of youth had passed" (117); "she did not blame Ned Currie and did not know what to blame" (117); and "an odd sense of relief came with this, her first bold attempt to face the fear that had become a part of her everyday life" (117). When Anderson moves to

Alice's life at twenty-five, he shows Alice losing her mother (who although older than Alice is fully engaged with living) to remarriage. Alice herself joins the Winesburg Methodist Church for fellowship, and in a feeble attempt at courtship, she allows Will Hurley, a drugstore clerk, to walk her home from Wednesday evening church services. But Alice is utterly unable to invite Will to stay with her or to call a new love into her barren life. The church and the man are of no help, Alice realizes; "I want to avoid being so much alone. If I am not careful I will grow unaccustomed to being with people" (118).

And then comes the "adventure" for which Alice Hindman's story is named, the event in her life that both demonstrates her grotesquerie and encapsulates the meaning of her life. One rainy night in the autumn of the year when she is twenty-seven, Alice tries to comfort herself with imaginings and dreams of happiness. She "took a pillow into her arms and held it tightly against her breasts. Getting out of bed, she arranged a blanket so that in the darkness it looked like a form lying between the sheets and, kneeling beside the bed, she caressed it, whispering words over and over, like a refrain" (118–19). The Ned Currie fantasy that she has held for the eleven years is no longer enough: "She did not want Ned Currie or any other man. She wanted to be loved, to have something answer the call that was growing louder and louder within her" (119). The call of repressed and irresistible desires lures Alice Hindman from her desperation into the "adventure" (119) of her life.

Suddenly frantically afraid of age and unloveliness, Alice runs naked out of her house, into the street and into the falling rain, feeling somehow that the rainwater will refresh and rejuvenate her. The falling rain is effective, as "not for years had she felt so full of youth and courage. She wanted to leap and run, to cry out, to find some other lonely human and embrace him" (119). One other human being, probably another very lonely one, does appear in the darkened Winesburg street. Alice, naked, calls to him, "Wait!" (119)—waiting, the act she has been performing for eleven years now. But this other person, the man the desperate Alice Hindman finds, is an old and rather deaf man, unable to answer her call, or to fulfill her desires, or perhaps even to see her in the evening's darkness. Dropping to the wet ground, humiliated by her own actions, Alice

Hindman literally crawls back into her house. Safe among the furniture of her lonely bedroom, she blockades her bedroom door with a dressing table, walling herself into her own room and her most private self. She weeps uncontrollably and, "turning her face to the wall, began trying to force herself to face bravely the fact that many people must live and die alone, even in Winesburg" (120).

Oh, yes, indeed, responds the superficial reader; certainly the grotesque people of Winesburg, Ohio, are doomed to live and die alone. But certainly, concludes the more thoughtful reader at the conclusion of the story "Adventure," all the world's people are doomed to live and to die alone, no matter how well they delude themselves with fantasies of closeness and intimate love. Nowhere else in *Winesburg, Ohio* does Anderson more movingly and fully unite his philosophy with his narrative technique than in the story of the tenderly pathetic and grotesque Alice.

"Respectability" is one of the important stories in the initiation of the youthful George Willard, but it also contains one of the most striking and extreme instances of the grotesquerie of human appearance and character.

In an unusual introduction, Anderson directly addresses the reader: "If you have lived in cities and have walked in the park on a summer afternoon"; and "had you been in the earlier years of your life a citizen of the village of Winesburg, Ohio" (121). The author then introduces Wash (for "Washington") Williams, who is likened to "a huge, grotesque kind of monkey, a creature with ugly, sagging, hairless skin below his eyes and a bright purple underbody" (121). Always dreadfully unclean—except for his always immaculate hands—Wash Williams, the most physically grotesque character in all of the stories, has for years been the dependable telegraph operator in Winesburg. The finer citizens of the town are disgusted by his filth and his omnipresent, malevolent misanthropy, for he clearly dislikes both women and men. Living at the New Willard House, to which he staggers home drunkenly each evening, Wash Williams becomes an object of curiosity to George, and they have several times almost come to conversation. George's recent walks about town with Belle

Carpenter inspire this disreputable telegraph operator to give George his most precious advice, his direst warning about life.

One night in darkness outside of town, sitting on some decaying railroad ties, Wash Williams (the name being ironic for this outwardly filthy man) tells George a story of hatred and loathing—a hatred and loathing so pure and so emotionally expressed that, to George, it seems that the voice telling the tale is that of a poet speaking life's truths. To the anxious George and to the expectant reader, the autobiography of Wash Williams is frightening and chilling.

Years ago, in the larger city of Dayton, Ohio, a youthfully clean, and physically and emotionally virginal young telegraph operator married a woman who "was tall and slender and had blue eyes and yellow hair" (123). The respectable daughter of a dentist, she joined her respectable and worshipful young husband in setting up a respectable home in the still larger city of Columbus, a home complete with the usual respectable furnishings and with a backyard especially for vegetable gardening.

In their first spring of gardening, young Wash Williams was digging with his spade and "turned up the black ground while she ran about laughing and pretending to be afraid of the worms I uncovered. Late in April came the planting. In the little paths among the seed beds she stood holding a paper bag in her hand. The bag was filled with seeds. A few at a time she handed me the seeds that I might thrust them into the warm, soft ground" (126). The imagery is that of another Adam and Eve, complete with their innocent original garden, and yet there is also the heated sexual imagery of postlapsarian human intercourse. In an even more courtly vision of innocent, youthful love, Wash Williams remembers of his garden: "There in the dusk in the spring evening I crawled along the black ground to her feet and groveled before her. I kissed her shoes and the ankles above her shoes. When the hem of her garment touched my face I trembled" (126). Perhaps such worship of a woman by a man soon became intolerable to her; perhaps she had not, as her husband had, remained virginal until marriage; or perhaps enthusiastic outdoor gardening does not equate with enthusiastic indoor lovemaking. For whatever reason, after two years of marriage, Wash Williams learns, his adored wife has taken three lovers who regularly come to her in their once-romantic honeymoon cottage. Consumed with a bitterness as intense as his virginal love had been, he quickly gives her all their money and sends her home, as rejected and damaged, to her respectable family in Dayton, Ohio.

And yet Wash Williams's embitterment is not, with this grave betrayal, complete, for one more episode completes and sets forever this man's misogyny. Wash, still in love with his unfaithful wife and summoned by his mother-in-law, probably for a reconciliation, visits her family home in Dayton. Sent to wait in the parlor—the most "respectable" room of the house—Wash hears argumentative words, and his wife is thrust naked into the room where he waits. Presumably he is to respond to her nakedness and in passion's heat reclaim her as his wife. Rightly blaming not the wife but the mother-in-law for this new and awful assault upon his ideals, Wash tries to beat the older woman to death. But like most desires in *Winesburg, Ohio,* this desire for just vengeance remains unfulfilled, for the mother-in-law dies of an unrelated fever a month after Wash's trauma in the parlor. Now the reader knows why Wash Williams is misanthropic and misogynistic, why he keeps his hands so immaculately clean of emotional and physical involvement and feels so cleanly righteous inwardly, yet neglects his filthy outward appearance. The reader learns, once more, that it is not only in Winesburg that traumatic events occur, events that can lead to psychological grotesquerie, for the "adventure" that ruins Wash's life takes place in Dayton, a city seemingly without the constrictions and catastrophes that supposedly occur only in such narrow, repressive towns as Winesburg.

"The Thinker" is the first of a series of four stories—the others being "Loneliness," " 'Queer' " and "Drink"—that deal with the quiet men and boys of Winesburg. The buried lives of the unobtrusive and unaggressive citizens are brought into contact with George Willard, Anderson's recurring character, so that the author may narrate their "adventures," their moments of epiphany.

"The Thinker" concerns the life of Seth Richmond, eighteen. Seth's father was killed in a street duel with a newspaper editor in Toledo, Ohio, after the newspaper editor had coupled the father's name flagrantly with that of a schoolteacher. Since then, Virginia Richmond reared her only child, Seth, in Winesburg. She has taught him to ignore all references to the dead father's imperfections and to think of him as having been a thoroughly good and gentle man. Perhaps it is Virignia's ignoring of the facts of life that has led her son into quietude and placidity. But his silence has brought the youth the sobriquet "the thinker," although behind Seth's quiescence there is neither high purpose nor especial cerebral activity.

As Wing Biddlebaum in "Hands" had to overlook an agricultural field to see people and events passing him by on the road of life, the roadway to Winesburg, Seth Richmond, who lives with his mother out of town at the end of Main Street, must from his isolated, once-grand home look from his distance at the road of life—that is, to see "wagon-loads of berry pickers—boys, girls, and women—going to the fields in the morning and returning covered with dust in the evening. . . . He regretted that he also could not laugh boisterously, shout meaningless jokes and make of himself a figure in the endless stream of moving, giggling activity that went up and down the road" (128).

And as the townspeople think (wrongly) of Seth, as he goes among them, as deliberative, measured, and deep in this thoughts, so his mother, unable to understand her unusual child, has an "almost unhealthy respect for the youth" (130). But "the truth was that the son thought with remarkable clearness and the mother did not" (130). To contrast Seth's maturity with his mother's naïveté, Anderson has the boy at sixteen run away from Winesburg and spend some days at a fairground and horse race. Virginia Richmond writes down the reproofs with which she will sting Seth's conscience upon his return. But on his homecoming he rationally explains that it was only his pride that set him on this most unsatisfactory and uncomfortable adventure, and the mother is silent, unable to address at all her son's wayward behavior.

The youth's contact with two of his Winesburg contemporaries—George Willard and Helen White—further reveals his nature and continues the narration of his "adventure." His relationship with George Willard, his longtime friend, is peculiar—seemingly of George's making and not Seth's, for George finds in the quiet boy a listener to hear of his dreams and plans. On the present evening in "The Thinker," Seth has walked silently among the citizens of Winesburg in quiet disgust. They are carrying on their meaningless and yet necessary daily pleasantries and banalities. Seth finds George in his room at the New Willard House, ready to maturely smoke a pipe and brag of trying to write a love story. Perhaps, George comments, he must be in love before he can execute a proper love story. Would Seth mind telling Helen White that George is in love with her? Seth is in no mood tonight to listen to George's bragging or to play Cupid for George's literary endeavors; further, disgusted by his additional useless and misused words, Seth leaves his friend and walks through Winesburg at dusk, only to witness again the clots of friendly folk who apparently belong to and constitute the wholeness and harmony of human society, yet who are removed, as if walled off, from the life of Seth Richmond: "feeling himself an outcast in his own town," Seth "began to pity himself, but a sense of the absurdity of his thoughts made him smile. In the end he decided that he was simply old beyond his years and not at all a subject for self-pity" (137).

But Seth Richmond's own interest in Helen White has just now been stirred by George's meretricious suggestion, so he walks to Banker White's mansion, where he finds Helen and invites her to walk with him. The two young people have been lifelong friends, and tonight Seth, after hearing so many wasted words from the people of Winesburg, somehow wants to say significant words to someone himself. On this pleasant summer evening they stroll quietly past a kissing man and woman and sit in the wooded garden that surrounds the Richmond house. In his economic description of this nighttime walk, Anderson brilliantly objectifies and dramatizes the buried life, the unconscious mind, of Seth Richmond.

As Seth and Helen walk toward his family home, he holds her hand and recalls to himself, scarcely consciously, an event of a few days before. Running an errand in the lovely country near Winesburg, he "had stopped beneath a sycamore tree and looked about him. A soft humming noise had greeted his ears. For a moment he had thought the tree must be the home of a swarm of bees" (140); then, "looking down, Seth had seen the bees everywhere all about him in the long grass. . . . The weeds were abloom with tiny purple blossoms and gave forth an overpowering fragrance. Upon the weeds the bees were gathered in armies, singing as they worked" (140). In the present, still holding Helen's hand, Seth remembers this wonderfully bucolic scene and imagines himself lying in the flowery grasses again, this time with Helen White at evening; then, in his imagined romantic scene, "a peculiar reluctance kept him from kissing her lips, but he felt he might have done that if he wished" (140). In the present, with the real-life Helen beside him, Seth immediately releases her hand, apparently unable to proceed, even in fancy, with kissing her. Unable to act upon his sexual impulses, he reverts to unusual behavior—braggart talking to Helen, of his having to grow up, of his having to amount to something in life, of his having to leave Winesburg immediately to get on with his new manhood.

And it seems that nature itself cooperates with Seth Richmond in his blustery talking, for great instances of thunder and lightning accompany his important words, promising heavy summer rain. "Helen White was impressed," narrates Anderson. "This boy is not a boy at all, but a strong, purposeful man" (141). But the more Seth talks instead of acts, the less enchanted Helen becomes with him, until Seth says words of good-bye forever, and Helen in "a wave of sentiment" pulls his head down to kiss him. But "the act was one of pure affection and cutting regret that some vague adventure that had been present in the spirit of the night would now never be realized" (142). Sensing that in Seth she is dealing with an adolescent and not, after all, with "a strong, purposeful man," Helen lets her hand fall and more or less sends Seth, as if he were a little boy, inside the house to his mother: "You go and talk with your mother. You'd better do that now" (142). Seth, "perplexed and puzzled by her action as he had been perplexed and puzzled by all of the life of the town out of which she had come" (142), ends his adventure (or, better, his lack of adventure) by walking toward his mother, who is domestically and maternally sewing by a lighted window. Seth knows that he will never leave Winesburg, but that he will never belong there, that he will forever be separate, that "when it comes to loving someone, it won't never be me. It'll be someone else—some fool—someone who talks a lot—someone like that George Willard" (142). There is no hint that Seth will ever again, in any way, seek close connection with another human being; his life will surely continue to be an absence of adventure, a presence of anomie.

"Loneliness" is one of Anderson's bleaker stories of the grotesque. For in it he allows the main character no hope of reconstructing destroyed illusions that could keep away the chill reality of solitude and desolation in Winesburg, Ohio. The culprit who unwittingly destroys the older man's possibility of warm illusion is George Willard, still athirst for the inside story of human life and here willing to dominate a weaker personality to get that story. The trauma that creates the grotesquerie in "Loneliness," as it did with Wing Biddlebaum in "Hands," happens to the protagonist far away from the little Ohio town, this time in the vastness of New York City.

Enoch Robinson spent his youth near Winesburg and took with him to New York, not only his dreams of becoming a painter, but the essence of his early life in Ohio. He lived with his mother outside of town on a side road off Trunion Pike, in a farmhouse the front blinds of which were always kept closed. When Enoch was young, he was a contemplative, dreaming fellow who tended to walk in the very middle of roads until he disrupted the ordinary traffic of life and was angrily shouted "out of the beaten track" (167). Solitary by nature and dangerous to himself when among adults, Enoch, narrates Anderson, "was always a child and that was a handicap to his worldly development. He never grew up and of course he couldn't understand people and he couldn't make people understand him. The child in him kept bumping against things, against actualities like money and sex and opinions" (167–68). True to his innocent nature, early in his fifteen-year stay in New York, Enoch is struck by a streetcar and lamed, giving him the almost-requisite physical difference of Anderson's grotesque characters.

This child-man, destined for failure both as an artist and in his personal relationships, has many adventures in New York. He becomes drunk enough to be taken by the police and receive a frightening lesson in sobriety; he is tempted into sexual adventure by a streetwalker but then is frightened away from her and is laughed at by her and by a passing male stranger. He goes about with other young would-be artists, but sputteringly inarticulate, he is unable to explain to them his intentions in his art; and he gradually becomes isolated in his room—a room, says

Anderson, "long and narrow like a hallway. . . . The story of Enoch is in fact the story of a room almost more than it is the story of a man" (168).

Just what Anderson intends to communicate to the reader through the spare description of Enoch's bare New York room, his personal space, long and narrow, is not entirely clear; but this room, hall-like and yet leading nowhere, becomes the setting for an imaginary life, with which the art student can comfortably cope: "With quick imagination he began to invent his own people to whom he could really talk and to whom he explained the things he had been unable to explain to living people" (170), "people of his own mind, people with whom he could really talk, people he could harangue and scold by the hour, servants, you see, to his fancy" (171).

Although he is solitary among his imagined playmates in his peculiar room, Enoch tries again to play games with real life, for he is visited by lust and loneliness and the desire "to touch actual flesh-and-bone people with his hands" (171). Thinking to satisfy his sexual urges and to play grown-up, he finds a more ordinary apartment; he marries the woman who sits conveniently near him in art class; and he begins to practice what he considers adult behavior—or, as Anderson writes, "He dismissed the essence of things and played with realities" (171). He illustrates advertisements for a living, he votes in elections, he reads a daily newspaper, he discusses possible government ownership of railroads, and he fathers two children—or at least, the author cannily suggests, his wife bears two children while she is married to Enoch.

But the childlike Enoch Robinson cannot long be happy playing at marriage and middle-class. Wishing once again to be alone with the playthings of his mind, he rerents the old, narrow apartment near Washington Square. When he fortuitously inherits money on the death of his mother back home, he gives his wife eight thousand dollars with which to divorce him and move to Connecticut and marry a real estate agent, that person most opposite to a dreamy artist. Then, safe again in his hall-like room, he repeoples his surroundings with the pliant comrades of his imagination.

But characters in *Winesburg, Ohio* are allowed little peaceful happiness, and events conspire, in the form of a very flesh-and-blood woman, to drive Enoch away from the city: "Something had to come into his world. Something had to drive him out of the New York room to live out his life an obscure, jerky little figure, bobbing up and down on the streets of an Ohio town at evening when the sun was going down behind the roof of Wesley Moyer's livery barn" (173).

This woman, who is simply a woman from next door and is possibly only seeking innocent relief from her own loneliness, repeatedly invades Enoch's sanctuary. By her huge and female adulthood, she comes to dominate his weak childishness, until he orders her away in uncontrolled, infantile rage. Unfortunately, he refers to his imagined playmates: "Then I began to tell her about my people, about everything that meant anything to me. I tried to keep quiet, to keep myself to myself, but I couldn't" (176). "A look" (176)—surely a look of recognition that she has been dealing with a nearly deranged person—comes into her eyes, and she leaves Enoch's now-polluted apartment: "Out she went through the door and all the life there had been in the room followed her out. She took all of my people away. They all went out through the door after her. That's the way it was" (177). Of all the sadness in *Winesburg, Ohio*, this is saddest: that Enoch Robinson has come back, desolate and totally alone, from New York to live out his years in Winesburg in a sparsely furnished room, that he somehow creates anew a consoling gathering of imaginary companions, and that by telling his story and his dreams to George Willard, he has once again destroyed his lonely solace. For at the end of "Loneliness" he says to himself, "I'm alone, all alone here. . . . It was warm and friendly in my room but now I'm all alone" (178).

That the Cowleys do not belong among the citizens of Winesburg is clear from the location of Cowley & Son's hardware store—not on the Main Street but on Maumee Street, near Voight's wagon shop and a horse-sheltering shed. The Cowleys, of " 'Queer,' " are indeed displaced persons, for a year ago, Ebenezer Cowley, the father of the family, sold his farmland and established the second (and scarcely needed) hardware business in Winesburg to follow that American dream of commercial success. His wife has died; the daughter is only mentioned and does not appear in the story; and Ebenezer himself is pathetically out of place with his long-worn but only good coat, his visible wen, his unwashed body, his storeful of useless and unneeded farm and shop supplies, and his all-purpose saying, "I'll be starched. . . . Well, well, I'll be washed and ironed and starched!" (193).

But it is Ebenezer's son, Elmer Cowley (both names hint at country origins), who is most unhappy in the town of Winesburg; and it is Elmer Cowley who is the grotesque character of " 'Queer.' " The quotation marks in the story title indicate that "queer" (as in "unusual" or "odd") is an epithet applicable, Elmer realizes, to all the Cowley family members. Elmer is described as pale, almost colorless in hair and skin, with pro-truding teeth and white-blue eyes—that is, he is slightly physically gro-tesque. Anderson illustrates the grotesquerie of Elmer Cowley in three ways: he shows his youthful rebellion against his nature and circum-stances, presumably for the first time in his life; he contrasts Elmer's character with that of three other Winesburg area residents (Ebenezer Cowley, Mook, a farmhand, and George Willard); and he presents George Willard as the object of Elmer Cowley's resentment, for George represents to the odd young man all those regular people who seem to fit so conveniently and comfortably into life in the Ohio town.

Elmer's rebellion comes one day when, trying awkwardly to thread his shoelaces (George Willard can be seen from the back room of the Cowley store), Elmer hears a traveling salesman foisting off unsalable items onto the gullible Ebenezer. Elmer takes a gun and orders the sales-man out of the store. Elmer cannot explain to his puzzled father this er-ratic, sudden, and dangerous uprising, his first rebellion against "queerness." Instead of receiving sympathy from a wise and understand-ing father for his outburst against oddness, Elmer receives from Ebenezer only the saying "I'll be washed and ironed and starched!" (193).

Frustrated by his inability to explain himself, Elmer madly runs out of Winesburg and into the countryside, where he had lived until a year ago and where he understood life and his place in it. As Elmer trudges along the rural road, he thinks: "I will not be queer—one to be looked at and listened to. . . . I'll be like other people. I'll show that George Willard. He'll find out. I'll show him!" (194). But George Willard, as the reader knows, has his own problems and concerns and has only passing interest in the strange young man whom he has occasionally seen on the streets of Winesburg.

When he arrives at the rural homeplace, Elmer finds himself almost happy as he talks to Mook, a half-witted farmhand who worked on this land when it was the Cowleys' and who has stayed on to work for the new owner. To Mook, Elmer has no trouble communicating his worries and his pleasures, for Mook is easy to talk to. Mook "believed in the intelligence of the animals that lived in the sheds with him, and when he was lonely held long conversations with the cows, the pigs, and even with the chickens that ran about the barnyard" (195). To Mook, Elmer explains at length the troubles that the Cowleys have encountered since their unwise move to town; how the money from the farmland is dwindling away in poor business practices; and most important of all, how Elmer feels rejected and alone and simply cannot fit into Winesburg: " 'In the evening, there in town, I go to the post office or to the depot to see the train come in, and no one says anything to me. Everyone stands around and laughs and they talk but they say nothing to me. Then I feel so queer that I can't talk either' " (197). Suddenly, he realizes the oddness of his present circumstances—that a "queer" one is talking seriously to a half-witted one. Elmer ends his harangue with: "I had to tell someone and you were the only one I could tell. I hunted out another queer one, you see. I ran away, that's what I did. I couldn't stand up to someone like that George Willard" (197). As Elmer runs back toward town, Mook confides in his animal friends that Elmer may hurt someone and concludes of the episode: "I'll be washed and ironed and starched" (197).

Elmer's rebellion is now concentrated even more firmly on George Willard. At eight on the same cold November evening, Elmer mysteriously summons the newspaper reporter to walk with him on the town streets. But when the time comes to talk, he cannot explain himself or his enormous rage. He orders George away, only to summon him again near midnight, when a freight train is leaving Winesburg for Cleveland. For Elmer has decided to steal some of his father's money, flee the town of his persecution, and go to a city whose vastness will both hide him and give him comfort: "He would get work in some shop and become friends with the other workmen and would be indistinguishable. Then he could talk and laugh. He would no longer be queer and would make friends. Life would begin to have warmth and meaning for him as it had for others" (199–200). But once again, when the train is ready to leave and George Willard is nearby and sleepily curious about Elmer for the second time that evening, Elmer can only thrust the stolen money onto George, beat mercilessly upon the reporter's breast, and incoherently proclaim: "I'll be washed and ironed and starched" (200). Leaving George Willard no wiser for his interrupted sleep and his pains, Elmer Cowley departs from Winesburg, crying to himself: "I guess I showed him. I ain't so queer. I guess I showed him I ain't so queer" (201). But carrying himself with himself, Elmer Cowley will forever be, wherever he may be, a social isolate, a "queer," a grotesque from Winesburg, Ohio.

"Drink," the fourth story about the usually quiet men and boys of Winesburg, concerns Tom Foster, a native of Cincinnati who was orphaned there and brought at sixteen to Winesburg by his quite elderly grandmother. She wants the youth to grow up in this peaceful, tiny village, which she left decades ago. The grandmother worries that the enlarged town of eighteen hundred people will not be right for Tom; but this youth, quiet and pleasant, would fit into any society, for everyone likes him, even the tough guys and prostitutes among whom he innocently lived in Cincinnati.

Tom Foster is not one of Anderson's more physically grotesque characters; small for his age and topped with unruly black hair, his head is larger than ordinary and his voice softer, but otherwise he is quite average, quite unobtrusive, and quite inoffensive. Enjoying an easy life in Winesburg, Tom survives by doing such jobs as cutting wood, mowing lawns, and picking strawberries. He most enjoys the quiet things about the town, fits into all groups of men and boys standing or sitting about to talk, and delights in such sensuous little things as the fresh-roasting coffee in Hern's grocery, the bedewed shiny stones in a handsome driveway, the sound of rain falling at night on tin roofs, and the power of a passing winter storm. But into his almost idyllic and carefree life must come some complication, and spring is the mischief that disrupts Tom's: "The trees along the residence streets of the town were all newly clothed in soft green leaves, in the gardens behind the houses men were puttering about in vegetable gardens, and in the air there was a hush, a waiting kind of silence very stirring to the blood" (216). On such a night even Tom Foster, who usually stays peacefully "in the shadow of the wall of life" (212), must have an adventure.

But all the eighteen-year-old youth really accomplishes on this sublime spring evening is to become drunk and think wondrous thoughts, perhaps for the first time in his life. Such drunkenness and such thinking do not at first seem important enough to be considered an adventure, or a revealing moment in a *Winesburg, Ohio* story. To understand the momentous importance to Tom Foster of this evening of drinking, the reader must recall an earlier adventure in Tom's life, an adventure that occurred when he was younger and living in a questionable district of Cincinnati.

Tom Foster's previous adventure was the occasion of his first temptation to sexual knowledge, when a prostitute in the district where he worked and lived invited the innocent boy to her room: "He never forgot the smell of the room nor the greedy look that came into the eyes of the woman. It sickened him and in a very terrible way left a scar on his soul. He had always before thought of women as quite innocent things, much like his grandmother, but after that one experience in the room he dismissed women from his mind" (215). Not only were women dismissed from Tom Foster's mind, but he seems to have banished all deep emotions and serious feelings, leaving in their absence the placid and amicable chap so well liked in Winesburg for his blandness and his unforward presence. But such emotional repression must have its eventual outlet, and Tom's drinking is the first expression of the denied emotion that he has buried so deep that he is not even aware of it.

On this fine spring evening Tom lets himself fantasize about Helen White, whom Seth Richmond and George Willard and perhaps other young men of the town have also admired. To Tom, this pretty young woman seems "a flame dancing in the air" and he himself "a little tree without leaves standing out sharply against the sky" (216). When, to his fancy, "she was a wind, a strong terrible wind," Tom is "a boat left on the shore of the sea by a fisherman" (216). Whatever importance should be

given to these images of active female force and passive male object is unclear; but after Tom has these daring thoughts, he goes out into the nighttime spring countryside near Winesburg to become gloriously drunk—
that is, when safely alone, to free his emotions from their traumatic
repression and to feel again something powerful, something forceful,
something active.

The adventure of drunkenness works for this youth, who may
henceforth be less divorced from life and its tearing and joyful emotions.
For, as he explains to a kindly and puzzled George Willard later the same
evening, as he is coming down from his drunken heights: "I wanted to
suffer, to be hurt somehow. I thought that was what I should do. I
wanted to suffer, you see, because everyone suffers and does wrong. . . .
It hurt me to do what I did and made everything strange. That's why I did
it. I'm glad, too. It taught me something, that's it, that's what I wanted.
Don't you understand? I wanted to learn things, you see. That's why I did
it" (219).

Like "Adventure," "The Untold Lie" is almost completely separable
from the other stories of *Winesburg, Ohio*. It is little concerned with
George Willard or the town of Winesburg and can stand alone as a short
story of great worth, although it lacks "Adventure's" dramatic impact.
"The Untold Lie" is hardly based on grotesquerie at all but is rather a
study in contrasts and cycles and is perhaps Anderson's most optimistic
philosophical fiction.

"The Untold Lie" is set in autumn near Winesburg, taking place in a
few hours in the lives of two farm workers—Hal Winters, a young man
who (like Shakespeare's Prince Hal?) cannot be tamed by outside forces
but who could tame himself to the bonds of ordinary social life, and Ray
Pearson, an older man who, long married and burdened with "half a
dozen thin-legged children" (202), has become thoroughly tamed to the
demands of marriage and fatherhood. The story is one of mostly silence,
as the two farmhands quietly crouch to shuck corn in a field lovely with
autumn's blazing colors. Ray and Hal work at their harvesting task almost automatically, until unexpectedly the younger man mutters:
"Tricked by Gad, that's what I was, tricked by life and made a fool of"

(204). Thus moved to express his smoldering anger, Hal continues: "Has a fellow got to do it? . . . Has he got to be harnessed up and driven through life like a horse?" (205). To his astonished companion Hal continues: "I've got Nell Gunther in trouble" (205); that is, on one of their courtship meetings he has impregnated the English teacher: "Perhaps you've been in the same fix yourself. I know what everyone would say is the right thing to do, but what do you say? Shall I marry and settle down?" (205).

Ray Pearson, thus startlingly appealed to for advice, cannot answer his young companion at all and walks wordlessly away from their common work, off across the fallow fields, where he is caught up by thoughts of the younger man's abrupt question about responsibility and freedom. Strangely, just such a dilemma occurred in Ray's youth: whether he should marry the woman who had so willingly gone walking in woods with him, or whether he should escape to the West Coast, where he might live freely and excitingly. As in other Anderson stories, this present moment of questioning of circumstances of long standing is assumed to be the first such mutiny in a character's life, his first need or opportunity to assert his individuality against the expectations of routine civilization.

Ray Pearson's silent self-questioning and potential insurrection gain dramatic impact when he goes to his bleak little tenant house, isolated among the rolling Ohio hills, where his shrewish wife and his half-dozen demanding children impatiently await him. There he is pushed into making a trip into Winesburg for food. Walking across a field toward the grocery stores, Ray is overcome by "the beauty of the country about Winesburg" (207) and suddenly "forgot all about being a quiet old farm hand and throwing off the torn overcoat began to run across the field. As he ran he shouted a protest against his life, . . . against everything that makes life ugly" (207). He recalls that when he was courting Minnie years ago, he promised her nothing; she had wanted sexual adventure as much as he, and biology had trapped him into marriage and parenthood.

Ray decides to warn Hal against making the same mistake, against completing the same cycle in human unhappiness. He runs madly and coatlessly across the plowed field toward the younger man, determined to be his oracle of escape and freedom and individualism. Then, as he runs, "he remembered his children and in fancy felt their hands clutching at him" (208); and suddenly seeing and coming upon Hal Winters, who is now dressed for courting and peacefully smoking a pipe of tobacco, Ray is unable to speak any words of his desperate warning. In fact, he says not a word, for Hal forestalls him with: "Well, never mind telling me anything. I'm not a coward and I've already made up my mind. . . . She didn't ask me to marry her. I want to marry her. I want to settle down and have kids" (208).

Thus does life cyclically and mechanically generate itself, Anderson seems to be saying—biology ensnares people into reproduction and childrearing, the prerequisites of civilization and progress. The price of this cycle and the social order that depends on it is, however, enormously high, and it is usually hopeless to elude. Even though Ray Pearson fails to say to Hal Winters anything at all, positive or negative, about being ambushed by fate into marriage—realizing that "whatever I told him would have been a lie" (209)—the reader is left to ponder whether Hal, in turn, will someday be faced with a questioning young male companion and be unable to advise either entrapment or escape, the only choices available to the individual as biology works its will. Optimistic? Yes. Pessimistic? Also yes. Truth, or lie? Both.

"Adventure" and "The Untold Lie" are both easy to enjoy and study singly, disjoined from the other stories in *Winesburg, Ohio*. But "The Strength of God" and "The Teacher" are two of Sherwood Anderson's greatest fictions, and they must be enjoyed and studied together, for they interrelate in event, in mood, and in style to form a unit that, in its completeness, demonstrates the quintessence of what *Winesburg, Ohio* is all about, of what grotesqueness and the buried life signify to Sherwood Anderson.

"The Strength of God" concerns the Reverend Curtis Hartman, who for ten years has been pastor of the Presbyterian Church of Winesburg, Ohio. The citizens are proud of his quiet, brown-bearded, and scholarly demeanor, and his stout wife, Sarah, grows "afire with secret pride" (147–48) as she rides with her respected husband in their carriage, although she is "worried lest the horse become frightened and run away" (148). But Curtis Hartman, who is in no way physically grotesque, has a hidden worry—he is secretly unhappy with his performance as minister of God: "he was much in earnest and sometimes suffered prolonged periods of remorse because he could not go crying the word of God in the highways and byways of the town. He wondered if the flame of the spirit really burned in him and dreamed of a day when a strong sweet new current of power would come like a great wind into his voice and his soul and the people would tremble before the spirit of God made manifest in him" (148). Each week, Hartman also worries at length about the sermon that he must deliver that Sunday morning, and frequently he comes to the little room in the tall bell tower of his church with anxiety, to meditate and to pray for the flame of the spirit.

This tall bell tower, freighted with its suggestively phallic shape, is central to the meaning of "The Strength of God," for here the events occur that ultimately convince Hartman that he has found "the strength of God" for which he has so fervently prayed. In the room are a table upon which rests the Bible that the minister devotedly studies and a small window made of stained glass, the design of which shows "Christ laying his hand upon the head of a child" (148). "The Strength of God" begins in summer, when the warm weather requires for comfort that the small stained-glass window be open. The minister is, one Sunday morning, shocked to look over the pages of his Bible, through the open window, and into the bedroom of the house next door to the church, where he sees a woman lying in bed while smoking and reading a book. So shocked is he by the worldliness of this woman who, on the Lord's day, would smoke, idle about her room, and avoid church, that probably for the first time in his life, "he went down into the pulpit and preached a long sermon without once thinking of his gestures or his voice. The sermon attracted unusual attention because of its power and clearness" (149). Merely from seeing a woman reading and smoking, the minister begins to find "the strength of God" for which he has been praying.

Seeing Kate Swift, the schoolteacher who lives with her mother next door to the church and who enjoys lying reading and smoking in her bed, is more important to the Reverend Curtis Hartman than anything that has ever happened to him. For the first time since his cold and passionless marriage to a very proper woman, he has been tempted to expand his horizons in regard to warm emotion and bodily attraction. Within a few days he wants to look again through his stained-glass window at the woman's body, but he knows to keep his spying secret. With a stone he "broke out a corner of the window and then locked the door and sat down at the desk before the open Bible to wait" (150). Interestingly, the portion of the stained-glass scene that he broke away is that which shows the heel of the boy being blessed by Christ. Indeed, the reader easily assumes, the Achilles' heel of the Reverend Curtis Hartman has been found and punctured by the arrow of quite ordinary lust. And again on the coming Sunday, the minister's sermon is personal, powerful, and cogent, for again with "the strength of God," he speaks to his congregation of personal temptation and godly forgiveness.

Anderson brilliantly handles Hartman's psychology. Over several weeks in summer and autumn, this developing character goes from horror at seeing the bare throat and white shoulders of a woman lying in bed to having a warm need to look again upon her throat and shoulders, to thanking God when she does not appear before his eyes to tempt him, to praying to be strong enough to repair the hole in the stained-glass window, to making feeble attempts at sexuality with his gelid wife, to abandoning his reticence about peeping at forbidden flesh, to rebelling and resolving to have and hold this wondrous female body just next door to the church.

For the "adventure," the telling instant in the character's life, the action moves to the darkest and most bitterly cold evening of the year. In the dark and unheated bell tower, frigid wind blows about the Reverend Hartman through the broken stained-glass window through which he has for months been peeping into the warm and lighted bedroom next door. Here the Reverend Hartman approaches both dying of physical illness (equated with the near-death of his soul) and a spiritual revelation of strength from God, for which he has earnestly been praying.

Into the prevailing imagery of coldness and warmth, Anderson introduces and interweaves images of darkness and light. The minister has come to see himself as more Hellenic than Hebraic, has had to spend long night hours in the coldness and darkness of his bell-tower room to await the entrance of the woman next door into her warm and well-lit bedroom. At the same time, he has begun to grope his way from the darkness of a cold and passionless marriage into the heated and enlightened passion of full human nature. When she appears in her bedroom, Kate Swift habitually wears a white nightgown that to Hartman should suggest angelity more than lust; and on this final night of peeping from the darkness, over his Bible, and through the stained-glass window, the vision he sees is indeed overwhelming and monumental. This night the woman does not appear in her lighted room until late, and instead of dressing in her white gown and lying quietly abed, she falls upon her bed completely naked and "lying face downward she wept and beat with her fists upon the pillow. With a final outburst of weeping she half arose and in the presence of the man who had waited to look and to think thoughts the woman of sin began to pray" (155). In the warm lamplight of her bedroom, Anderson writes, "her figure, slim and strong, looked like the figure of the boy in the presence of the Christ on the leaded window" (155).

In the bell tower the Bible dramatically falls to the floor as the minister rises from his seated position. When the light finally goes out in the unhappy woman's bedroom, the excited minister eagerly breaks the rest of the stained-glass window with his fist, thinking that his season of temptation is over and that he has found the strength of God in the body of a woman. The reader is left to wonder whether the minister is deluding himself that he has found the light of happiness or the continuing darkness of a new if godly self delusion.

The first thing to say about "The Teacher" is that Kate Swift, the object of the Reverend Hartman's desire in "The Strength of God," in this her own story is absolutely unaware of either her accessibility or her meaning to the peeping eyes of the preacher. In "The Strength of God" the reader learns, through Curtis Hartman, some information about Kate—specifically, that "the school teacher was thirty years old and had a neat trim-looking figure"; that she "had few friends and bore a reputation of having a sharp tongue"; that "she had been to Europe and had lived for two years in New York City" (149). Otherwise, in "The Strength of God," the woman next door to the church who is so addictive and almost liberating to the repressed preacher could have been any attractive Winesburg woman who likes occasionally to smoke and to read in bed.

In "The Teacher" Anderson does not present a great deal of new information about Kate Swift. She lives with her widowed mother, we learn, and her health is not good, as she is in some danger of losing her hearing. When seen close, Kate Swift is neither physically beautiful nor especially physically grotesque: "Her complexion was not good and her face was covered with blotches that indicated ill health" (160); yet to an observer who sees her walking purposefully on the coldest, darkest night of the year, "alone in the night in the winter streets she was lovely. Her back was straight, her shoulders square, and her features were as the features of a tiny goddess on a pedestal in a garden in the dim light of a summer evening" (160).

In "The Teacher," Anderson does expand upon the "sharp tongue" reference to her in "The Strength of God," for "there was something biting and forbidding in the character of Kate Swift." Since her return from Europe or New York five years ago, she has been "silent, cold and stern, and yet in an odd way very close to her pupils" in the schoolroom (161); George Willard is a recent graduate of the school. Only occasionally does Kate break from her iciness to tell to her pupils charming but seemingly irrelevant stories about such people as Charles Lamb and Benvenuto Cellini, only to immediately return to coldness and sternness. But since Anderson is more interested in the buried life of his characters than in their outward appearance and behavior, he confides to the reader about Kate Swift that "in reality she was the most eagerly passionate soul among them, and more than once, in the five years since she had come back from her travels to settle in Winesburg and become a school teacher, had been compelled to go out of the house and walk half through the night fighting out some battle raging within" (162). In the past, her battles with her own passionate nature have usually been settled by cold walks in the street; but in the present "adventure" of Kate Swift, Kate has a new problem, one perhaps not soluble by the usual vigorous exercise: her infatuation and lust for George Willard.

In consonance with the imagery of light and darkness and of

warmth and coldness in "The Strength of God," Anderson in "The Teacher" presents Kate's hot and hidden nature, usually bound down under her icy exterior, as emerging to focus on George Willard. On this particular night, so separately important to the Reverend Curtis Hartman and to the young newspaper reporter, "Kate Swift's mind was ablaze with thoughts of George Willard" (162); "in something he had written as a school boy she thought she had recognized the spark of genius and wanted to blow on the spark" (162–63). Thus for her "adventure," the incident that marks her epiphany, Kate Swift leaves the huge base-burner stove in her mother's warm and well-lighted house to face the bitterly cold darkness of January and to end up with her former pupil in the well-lighted and well-heated office of the *Eagle*. There she ostensibly lectures him about writing creatively from life after knowing about life, but in reality she is drawn toward his boyish good looks and his manhood. As she is about to leave, "in the warm little office the air became suddenly heavy and the strength went out of her body" (165). She lets herself fall into the young man's ready arms, but then in sudden reluctance or sudden passion beats upon his face and then runs away into the cold night.

Now the reader understands why the schoolteacher is so late to appear in her bedroom while Curtis Hartman waits in his freezing, dark bell tower; why she throws herself naked onto the bed and beats her pillow in her lighted, warm bedroom; and why she finally kneels on her bed—naked, slim and boylike—to pray. The reader can only speculate about the substance of her prayer; most likely, she prays, like Alice Hindman in "Adventure," that she herself will have the strength of God not to seduce a young student, that she will have the fortitude to learn to live and die alone, even in Winesburg, Ohio.

The reader who enjoys the stories in *Winesburg, Ohio* and who appreciates Anderson's narrative purposes and techniques might well wish for more, but Anderson wrote no more fiction about Winesburg, Ohio, and left for his masterpiece only the twenty-one stories published in the little yellow book of 1919. Why there are no more Winesburg stories is unclear, for it is unlikely that the author tired of them; more likely, he had to move on to new material. It is certain that he did have more Winesburg stories worth the telling, for on close examination of the stories that were written, there are intriguing references to other grotesque characters in the imaginary town.

These characters include Tom Willy and his birthmarked hands in "The Philosopher" (49); the once red-haired Bentley spinster who so adoringly rears David Hardy in "Godliness," who speaks to the sleeping boy the romantic thoughts forbidden to her, and who becomes "ecstatically happy" (79) when his hand brushes her face in his sleep; Turk Smollett, "the half dangerous old wood chopper whose peculiarities added so much of color to the life of the village" (137) and whose boisterous social acceptance in "The Thinker" offends Seth Richmond; Mook, the half-witted farmhand who in " 'Queer' " talks to the animals and shares a warm outdoor fire with the distraught Elmer Cowley (195–97); the pipe-smoking grandmother of Tom Foster in "Drink," who in advanced age lovingly tells her young grandson, "When you get ready to die then I will die also" (214); and Hop Higgins, the town's night watchman, who, on that cold January night in "The Teacher," peacefully dozes before the stove in the hotel office and dreams of a career raising ferrets (139).

One may regret that Sherwood Anderson did not write the stories of these and other surely interesting grotesques among the residents of Winesburg; but he did not, and the reader is encouraged to pursue later volumes of stories written by this author: *The Triumph of the Egg* (1921), *Horses and Men* (1923), and *Death in the Woods* (1933). In these three volumes are many stories, some about grotesques, that individually rival the best of the *Winesburg, Ohio* stories—stories that on their own are interesting and well enough fashioned to shock the careful reader with their beauty and worth.

Notes and References

1. The best discussion of Sherwood Anderson's life from his birth in 1876 through his move to Chicago in 1913 is William A. Sutton, *The Road to Winesburg: A Mosaic of the Imaginative Life of Sherwood Anderson* (Metuchen, N.J.: Scarecrow Press, 1972). The best biography of Anderson's whole life is Kim Townsend, *Sherwood Anderson* (Boston: Houghton Mifflin, 1987).

2. For a thorough discussion of Chicago during Anderson's years there, see Kenny J. Williams, *A Storyteller and a City: Sherwood Anderson's Chicago* (DeKalb: Northern Illinois University Press, 1988).

3. Two good discussions of Anderson's place in the Chicago Renaissance are Bernard Duffey, *The Chicago Renaissance in American Letters* (East Lansing: Michigan State College Press, 1954), and Dale Kramer, *Chicago Renaissance: The Literary Life in the Midwest, 1900–1930* (New York: Appleton-Century, 1966).

4. *Sherwood Anderson's Memoirs: A Critical Edition*, ed. Ray Lewis White (Chapel Hill: University of North Carolina Press, 1969), 352–53. For other comments from Anderson on the composition of the Winesburg stories, see this edition of his memoirs, pp. 22, 237–38, 341, 346–53, 412–18, and 510.

5. A good discussion of Anderson's life while he was writing *Winesburg, Ohio* is William Louis Phillips, "Sherwood Anderson's *Winesburg, Ohio*: Its Origins, Composition, Technique, and Reception" (Ph.D. diss., University of Chicago, 1949), which is summarized in William L. Phillips, "How Sherwood Anderson Wrote *Winesburg, Ohio*," *American Literature* 23 (1951): 7–30. The best description of Anderson's story manuscripts and the probable state of their composition is Ray Lewis White, "The Manuscripts of *Winesburg, Ohio*," *Winesburg Eagle* 11 (1985): 4–10; "*Winesburg, Ohio*: The Story Titles," *Winesburg Eagle* 10 (1984): 6–7; "*Winesburg, Ohio*: The Table of Contents," *Notes on Modern American Literature* 8 (1984): 1–4; and "*Winesburg, Ohio*: The Unique Alternate Draft of 'Nobody Knows,'" *Winesburg Eagle* 8 (1982): 3–5.

6. "The Rabbit-Pen," *Harper's* 129 (1914): 207–10.

7. For a discussion of the American short story as written when Anderson was composing *Winesburg, Ohio*, see Ray Lewis White, *Index to "Best American Short Stories" and "O. Henry Prize Stories"* (Boston: G. K. Hall, 1988), 5–15, 63–74.

8. *Sherwood Anderson's Memoirs*, 22.

9. Ibid., 177.

10. Ibid., 349.

11. Ibid., 467.

12. "A Gutter Would Be Spoon River," *New York Sun*, 1 June 1919, 3.

13. "Winesburg, Ohio," *New York World*, 1 June 1919, sec. E, p. 6.

14. Heywood Broun, "Winesburg, Ohio," *New York Tribune*, 31 May 1919, 10.

15. Wallace Smith, "Civilian Communique," *Chicago Daily News*, 3 September 1919, 6.

16. Anon., "Winesburg, Ohio," *Springfield Republican*, 20 July 1919, 15.

17. Maxwell Anderson, "A Country Town," *New Republic* 19 (25 June 1919): 260.

18. W. S. B., "Ohio Small Town Life," *Boston Transcript*, 11 June 1919, 6.

19. Hart Crane, "Sherwood Anderson," *Pagan* 4 (September 1919): 60–61.

20. Idwal Jones, "Winesburg, Ohio," *San Francisco Chronicle*, 31 August 1919, sec. S, p. 6.

21. Llewellyn Jones, "The Unroofing of Winesburg," *Friday Literary Review*, 20 June 1919, 9.

22. H. L. Mencken, "Novels, Chiefly Bad," *Smart Set* 59 (August 1919): 140, 142.

23. J. V. A. Weaver, "Sherwood Anderson," *Chicago Daily News*, 11 June 1919, 12.

24. Ray Lewis White, "*Winesburg* in Translation," *Ohioana Quarterly* 19 (Summer 1976): 58–60.

25. The standard discussion is Anthony Channell Hilfer, *The Revolt from the Village, 1915–1930* (Chapel Hill: University of North Carolina Press, 1969).

26. The standard discussion is Charles Child Walcutt, *American Literary Naturalism, a Divided Stream* (Minneapolis: University of Minnesota Press, 1956).

27. The standard discussion is Frederick J. Hoffman, *Freudianism and the Literary Mind*, 2d ed. (Baton Rouge: Louisiana State University Press, 1957).

28. This discussion of chronology appeared in altered form in Ray Lewis White, "Of Time and *Winesburg, Ohio*: An Experiment in Chronology," *Modern Fiction Studies* 25, no. 4 (Winter 1979–80): 658–66.

Selected Bibliography

Primary Works

Windy McPherson's Son. New York and London: John Lane, 1916.

Marching Men. New York and London: John Lane, 1917.

Mid-American Chants. New York and London: John Lane, 1918.

Winesburg, Ohio. New York: B. W. Huebsch, 1919.

Poor White. New York: B. W. Huebsch, 1920.

The Triumph of the Egg. New York: B. W. Huebsch, 1921.

Many Marriages. New York: B. W. Huebsch, 1923.

Horses and Men. New York: B. W. Huebsch, 1923.

A Story Teller's Story. New York: B. W. Huebsch, 1924.

Dark Laughter. New York: Boni and Liveright, 1925.

Sherwood Anderson's Notebook. New York: Boni and Liveright, 1926.

Tar: A Midwest Childhood. New York: Boni and Liveright, 1926.

A New Testament. New York: Boni and Liveright, 1927.

Hello Towns! New York: Horace Liveright, 1929.

Perhaps Women. New York: Horace Liveright, 1931.

Beyond Desire. New York: Liveright, 1932.

Death in the Woods. New York: Liveright, 1933.

No Swank. Philadelphia: Centaur Press, 1934.

Puzzled America. New York and London: Charles Scribner's Sons, 1935.

Kit Brandon. New York and London: Charles Scribner's Sons, 1936.

Plays: Winesburg and Others. New York: Charles Scribner's Sons, 1937.

Sherwood Anderson's Memoirs. New York: Harcourt, Brace, 1942.

The Sherwood Anderson Reader. Edited by Paul Rosenfeld. Boston: Houghton Mifflin, 1947.

The Portable Sherwood Anderson. Edited by Horace Gregory. New York: Viking Press, 1949.

Letters of Sherwood Anderson. Edited by Howard Mumford Jones and Walter B. Rideout. Boston: Little, Brown, 1953.

Winesburg, Ohio. Edited by Malcolm Cowley. New York: Viking Press, 1960; New York: Penguin, 1976.

Sherwood Anderson: Short Stories. Edited by Maxwell Geismar. New York: Hill and Wang, 1962.

"Winesburg, Ohio": Text and Criticism. Edited by John H. Ferres. New York: Viking Press, 1966.

Return to Winesburg. Edited by Ray Lewis White. Chapel Hill: University of North Carolina Press, 1967.

"Sherwood Anderson's Memoirs": A Critical Edition. Edited by Ray Lewis White. Chapel Hill: University of North Carolina Press, 1969.

"A Story Teller's Story": A Critical Text. Edited by Ray Lewis White. Cleveland: Press of Case Western Reserve University, 1969.

"Tar: A Midwest Childhood"—a Critical Text. Edited by Ray Lewis White. Cleveland: Press of Case Western Reserve University, 1971.

The Buck Fever Papers. Edited by Welford Dunaway Taylor. Charlottesville: University Press of Virginia, 1971.

Sherwood Anderson / Gertrude Stein: Correspondence and Personal Essays. Edited by Ray Lewis White. Chapel Hill: University of North Carolina Press, 1972.

"Marching Men": A Critical Text. Edited by Ray Lewis White. Cleveland: Press of Case Western Reserve University, 1972.

The "Writer's Book" by Sherwood Anderson: A Critical Edition. Edited by Martha Mulroy Curry. Metuchen, N.J.: Scarecrow Press, 1975.

France and Sherwood Anderson: Paris Notebook, 1921. Edited by Michael Fanning. Baton Rouge: Louisiana State University Press, 1976.

Sherwood Anderson: The Writer at His Craft. Edited by Jack Salzman, David D. Anderson, and Kichinosuke Ohashi. Mamaroneck, N.Y.: Paul P. Appel, 1979.

Complete Works of Sherwood Anderson. Edited by Kichinosuke Ohashi. 21 volumes. Kyoto: Rinsen, 1982.

The Teller's Tales. Edited by Frank Gado. Schenectady: Union College Press, 1983.

Sherwood Anderson: Selected Letters. Edited by Charles E. Modlin. Knoxville: University of Tennessee Press, 1984.

Letters to Bab: Sherwood Anderson to Marietta D. Finley, 1916–33. Edited by William A. Sutton. Urbana: University of Illinois Press, 1985.

The Sherwood Anderson Diaries, 1936–1941. Edited by Hilbert H. Campbell. Athens: University of Georgia Press, 1987.

Sherwood Anderson: Early Writings. Edited by Ray Lewis White. Kent and London: Kent State University Press, 1989.

Sherwood Anderson's Love Letters to Eleanor Copenhaver Anderson. Edited by Charles E. Modlin. Athens: University of Georgia Press, 1989.

Secondary Works

Books

Anderson, David D., ed. *Critical Essays on Sherwood Anderson.* Boston: G. K. Hall, 1981. An anthology by various scholars, with several essays on *Winesburg, Ohio.*

————. *Sherwood Anderson: An Introduction and Interpretation.* New York: Holt, Rinehart & Winston, 1967. A brief and sympathetic reading of Anderson's major writings.

————, ed. *Sherwood Anderson: Dimensions of His Literary Art.* East Lansing: Michigan State University Press, 1976. Essays by various scholars for the Anderson centennial.

Appel, Paul P., ed. *Homage to Sherwood Anderson: 1876–1941.* Mamaroneck, N.Y.: Paul P. Appel, 1970. A reprint of the 1941 issue of *Story,* dedicated to essays on Anderson just after his death, including some new letters.

Bruyère, Claire. *Sherwood Anderson: L'Impuissance Créatrice.* Paris: Klincksieck, 1985. Concerns Anderson's drive to express art that to him is almost inexpressible. (Written in French.)

Burbank, Rex. *Sherwood Anderson.* New York: Twayne Publishers, 1964. A general outline of Anderson's early works.

Campbell, Hilbert H., and Charles E. Modlin, eds. *Sherwood Anderson: Centennial Studies.* Troy, N.Y.: Whitson, 1976. Essays by various scholars in celebration of Anderson's centennial.

Chase, Cleveland. *Sherwood Anderson.* New York: R. M. McBride, 1927.

Fagin, N. Bryllion. *The Phenomenon of Sherwood Anderson: A Study in American Life.* Baltimore: Rossi-Bryn, 1927.

Howe, Irving. *Sherwood Anderson.* New York: William Sloan Associates, 1951. A generally negative reading of Anderson's works, except for *Winesburg, Ohio* and a few other stories.

Rideout, Walter B., ed. *Sherwood Anderson: A Collection of Critical Essays.* Englewood Cliffs, N.J.: Prentice-Hall, 1974. An anthology by various hands, with some material about *Winesburg, Ohio.*

Schevill, James. *Sherwood Anderson: His Life and Work.* Denver: University of Denver Press, 1951. The first biography; an admiring and germinal study.

Sutton, William A. *The Road to Winesburg: A Mosaic of the Imaginative Life of Sherwood Anderson.* Metuchen, N.J.: Scarecrow Press, 1972. A standard, detailed study of Anderson's life through the writing of *Winesburg, Ohio.*

Taylor, Welford Dunaway. *Sherwood Anderson.* New York: Ungar, 1977.

Townsend, Kim. *Sherwood Anderson.* Boston: Houghton Mifflin, 1987. The most recent attempt to cover Anderson's life; quite useful and more extensive than previous biographies.

Weber, Brom. *Sherwood Anderson.* Minneapolis: University of Minnesota Press, 1964. A brief introduction to the writer and his major work.

White, Ray Lewis, ed. *Sherwood Anderson: Essays in Criticism.* Chapel Hill: University of North Carolina Press, 1966. The first anthology of various essays and book reviews about Anderson, some regarding *Winesburg, Ohio.*

Williams, Kenny J. *A Storyteller and a City: Sherwood Anderson's Chicago.* DeKalb: Northern Illinois University Press, 1988. A detailed and expert study of the author and the city where he wrote *Winesburg, Ohio.*

Bibliographies

Sheehy, Eugene P., and Kenneth A. Lohf, eds. *Sherwood Anderson: A Bibliography.* Los Gatos, Cal.: Talisman Press, 1960. A useful list of works by Anderson; less useful and now quite outmoded list of secondary studies.

White, Ray Lewis. *Sherwood Anderson: A Reference Guide.* Boston: G. K. Hall, 1977. The most comprehensive secondary bibliography, through 1975.

Articles

Bredahl, A. Carl. " 'The Young Thing Within': Divided Narrative and Sherwood Anderson's *Winesburg, Ohio.*" *Midwest Quarterly* 27 (1986): 422–37. *Winesburg, Ohio* as a new form, neither novel nor story collection.

Bresnahan, Roger J. "The 'Old Hands' of Winesburg." *Midwestern Miscellany* 11 (1983): 19–27. The use of hands as symbolic and actual forces in the stories.

Cowan, James C. "The *Pharmakos* Figure in Modern American Stories of Physicians and Patients." *Literature and Medicine* 6 (1987): 94–109. The use of physicians and healing in the stories.

Selected Bibliography

Enniss, Stephen C. "The Implied Community of *Winesburg, Ohio.*" *Old Northwest* 11 (1985): 51–60. Daily life going on around the grotesques in the stories.

Hurd, Thaddeus B. "Fun in Winesburg." *Midwestern Miscellany* 11 (1983): 28–39. Actual daily life in Clyde, Ohio, in the 1880s.

Lowry, Jon S. "The Arts of Winesburg and Bidwell, Ohio." *Twentieth Century Literature* 23 (1977): 53–66. Anderson's characters both escaping and returning to the small town.

O'Neill, John. "Anderson Writ Large: 'Godliness' in *Winesburg, Ohio.*" *Twentieth Century Literature* 23 (1977): 67–83. The four-part "Godliness" fits in with the collected stories better than has previously been thought.

Papinchak, Robert Allen. "Something in the Elders: The Recurrent Imagery in *Winesburg, Ohio.*" *Winesburg Eagle* 9 (1983): 1–7. Patterns of symbols coordinate rather than isolate clusters of meaning.

Park, Martha M. "How Far from Emerson's Man of One Idea to Anderson's Grotesques?" *College Language Association Journal* 20 (1977): 374–79. The possibility that Anderson borrowed from Emerson the idea of "truths" distorting character.

Rigsbee, Sally Adair. "The Feminine in *Winesburg, Ohio.*" *Studies in American Fiction* 9 (1981): 233–44. Lack of communication due to loss of the "feminine" qualities in life.

Shilstone, Frederick W. "Egotism, Sympathy, and George Willard's Development as Poet in *Winesburg, Ohio.*" *West Virginia University Philological Papers* 28 (1982): 105–13. Experiencing the grotesques leads the main character toward poethood.

Stouck, David. "*Winesburg Ohio* as a Dance of Death." *American Literature* 48 (1977): 525–42. The recurrent use of death imagery and deaths occasions the dark aspects of the stories.

Sykes, Robert H. "The Identity of Anderson's Fantastical Farmer." *Studies in Short Fiction* 18 (1981): 79–82. An American inventor in DeKalb, Illinois, as model for "Godliness."

White, Ray Lewis. "The Manuscripts of *Winesburg, Ohio.*" *Winesburg Eagle* 11 (1985): 4–10. A technical description of the stories in Anderson's handwritten form.

————. "Mencken's Lost Review of *Winesburg, Ohio.*" *Notes on Modern American Literature* 2 (1978): 1–3. An appreciative, previously unknown review by the American satirist.

————. "Of Time and *Winesburg, Ohio*: An Experiment in Chronology." *Modern Fiction Studies* 25 (1979–80): 658–66. The life of the main character as a figure of initiation.

_____. "Sherwood Anderson and the Real Winesburg, Ohio." *Winesburg Eagle* 12 (1987): 1–4. The author's response to a complaint from a preacher in the actual town.

_____. "Socrates in *Winesburg*." *Notes on Modern American Literature* 10 (1986): 3–6. A possible source for the situation and lecture in "Hands."

_____. "*Winesburg* in 1919: The Publisher's Catalog Copy." *Winesburg Eagle* 3 (1978): 3–4. Advertising copy for the book from B. W. Huebsch, the publisher.

_____. "*Winesburg* in Translation: Ohio in the World." *Ohioana Quarterly* 19 (1976): 58–60. Worldwide versions of the book in many languages.

_____. "*Winesburg, Ohio:* A Unique 1919 Ohio Review." *Ohioana Quarterly* 22 (1979): 12–13. The only review at publication from the state of Ohio.

_____. "*Winesburg, Ohio:* First-Impression Errors." *Papers of the Bibliographical Society of America* 71 (1977): 222–23. Marks distinguishing the very first copies of the book.

_____. "*Winesburg, Ohio:* First Printings, Variants, and Errors." *Winesburg Eagle* 10 (1985): 1–3. Additional identifying marks of the first four printings of the book.

_____. "*Winesburg, Ohio:* A Lost Chicago Review." *Winesburg Eagle* 2 (1977): 2. Hitherto unknown commentary from Chicago, where Anderson was living in 1919.

_____. "*Winesburg, Ohio:* The Earliest Non-English-Language Review." *Winesburg Eagle* 3 (1978): 2–3. A Swedish-language review from 1919.

_____. "*Winesburg, Ohio:* The Story Titles." *Winesburg Eagle* 10 (1984): 6–7. Anderson's changes in titles as he completed the stories.

_____. "*Winesburg, Ohio:* The Table of Contents." *Notes on Modern American Literature* 8 (1984): 1–4. Anderson's changing arrangement of the stories for book publication.

_____. "*Winesburg, Ohio:* The Unique Alternate Draft of 'Nobody Knows.' " *Winesburg Eagle* 8 (1982): 3–5. A hitherto unnoticed handwritten version of one of the Winesburg stories—so far the only such alternate draft found.

Anderson Journal

The Winesburg Eagle: The Official Publication of the Sherwood Anderson Society (1975–). Edited by Charles E. Modlin and Hilbert H. Campbell, Department of English, Virginia Polytechnic Institute and State University, Blacksburg, Virginia.

Index

About the Author

Ray Lewis White, distinguished professor of English at Illinois State University, spent his early years in the Virginia Highlands, where Sherwood Anderson spent the last years of his life. A graduate of Emory & Henry College and the University of Arkansas, he is the author of many books about Anderson, including editions of the writer's three memoirs, his correspondence with Gertrude Stein, his writings for a country newspaper, and his earliest business and creative works. White's many articles on Anderson include numerous studies of *Winesburg, Ohio,* both historical and critical.

White has published books on the American short story and on Gore Vidal, Gertrude Stein, Alice B. Toklas, Günter Grass, Heinrich Böll, Pär Lagerkvist, and Arnold Zweig. He has published articles on Stein, John Steinbeck, Nathanael West, Ben Hecht, Willard Motley, Eldridge Cleaver, Evan S. Connell, Jr., F. Scott Fitzgerald, William H. Gass, Wallace Stevens, Zelda Fitzgerald, Margaret Mitchell, Carl Van Vechten, John Dos Passos, Mikhail Sholokhov, Raja Rao, Kawabata Yasunari, and R. K. Narayan.